The Apostles' Doctrine

by Robert E. Pate

Manufactured in the U.S.A.

ISBN 0-615-12608-1

Edited by Connie Pettersen
Cover by Sherry Bjerke
Cover Illustration by Samuel Nisenson

Published by Robert E. Pate
PO Box 62
Eau Claire, WI 54702
Fax 715-830-0453

Printed by Documation, LLC

Some of the names used in this book are fictitious.

All scripture used in this book is King James version and has been modified for clarity and easy understanding.

Table of Contents

Introduction

My dad moved from the Midwest to San Francisco when I was three years old. Most of my childhood years were spent growing up in San Francisco. My mother was a committed Pentecostal Christian. I remember going to church with my mother. I attended Sunday school class and after that I would go into the main auditorium, or as they called it, "the Sanctuary." I remember there was a lot of commotion like clapping, dancing, and people speaking in tongues. I never thought much about this. My mother always wanted to sit down in front with me and when the invitation was given, she would always bend over and say, "Bob, would you like to give your heart to Jesus." I always thought, why would I like to give my *heart* to Jesus. Sometimes my mother would just give me a little nudge with her elbow. I was scared to death to go to what they called the Altar and give my heart to Jesus.

One Sunday morning during the main service, my mother practically pushed me into the aisle during the invitation. So I kind of went stumbling down to the altar to give my heart to Jesus. I was about seven years old. I think I might have shed a tear or two, not because I was repentant, but because I was scared to death. I remember the preacher came over to me and put his hand on my head and said, "God bless you, Bobby!" My mother couldn't wait to buy my baptismal outfit.

Two or three Sundays later I was baptized. I didn't have the slightest idea what that was all about. Everybody in the church saw it happen and there was quite a commotion that took place. My mother said that now that I was a Christian, I should act like one. I think that was what it was really all about. I was curious about Christ, but that was as far as it went.

I remember that my mother had this real big Bible with lots of colored pictures in it. I remember one I especially liked was, "Daniel in the Lion's Den" and then there was a picture of Jesus sitting with the children gathered around him. His hand was on their head and I remember thinking, "well, maybe he's okay if he likes kids." I would go into the bedroom where my mother kept her Bible and look through it. I especially liked looking at the pictures. I never wanted her to see me doing this, because then she might think that I was becoming committed, so I always did it secretly.

My mother believed in visions and revelations. One time she claimed that her dead sister was floating over her bed and was trying to talk to her. After that she went to see a spiritualist to see if she could communicate with her dead sister. She started attending spiritualist meetings quite frequently until one Sunday afternoon she came home, laid down on the bed to rest, and all of a sudden the bed began to shake violently and the closet door started banging back and forth. I guess it half scared her to death and she didn't go back to the spiritualist meetings anymore after that.

I remember later on when I was a teenager, some of my friends wanted to go to another town and attend an Oral Roberts meeting. I decided that I would go with them – not to see Oral Roberts, but because I wanted to be with my friends. We sat right down in front. My friends were boasting about all the people that Oral Roberts had healed. I was almost to the point where I wished that I had something wrong with me so I could be healed. I was very skeptical, though, as to whether Oral Roberts could really heal anyone.

Finally the healing part of the service began. People lined up, some on crutches, some in wheel chairs; they all looked pretty bad

I thought to myself if these people really get healed, I'm going to become a believer.

The first one in line was an older guy who was on crutches. When he got up to Oral Roberts, Oral laid his hands on his head and said something in tongues rather feverishly. The old guy threw his crutches down and said, "Praise God, I've been healed." He went limping off without his crutches. I thought to myself, "If this guy's really been healed, why is he limping?"

I never saw one person in that line that I thought had been healed. Some people would jump up out of their wheelchairs and stagger around for a while, and later on they were back in their wheelchairs. I thought to myself, "Oral Roberts is a fraud." Later, on the way home, I expressed this to my friends. I thought they were going to throw me out of the car. How could I say such a terrible thing about Oral Roberts! I learned that people are very sensitive about their religious beliefs. This really turned me off towards Christianity. I thought to myself, "How could anybody be so stupid to think that Oral Roberts had the power to heal people. The people that did claim they were healed always had some internal problem so you couldn't tell if they were healed or not. If I could have seen an arm or even a finger replaced that had been cut off or amputated, I might have been a believer, but nothing like that had happened. I thought to myself, if this is really about Jesus Christ, everyone would be healed. I remembered some of what I had been taught in Sunday School that Jesus healed people, but he healed them completely and there was no partial healing or patch-up healing. I was about 16 years old when this took place, but I was old enough to know that there was something wrong with this religion. I didn't know exactly what it was, and I didn't exactly care. The next 18 years of my life I lived knowing that there was a Jesus Christ, but not really caring.

When I was 33, one Sunday afternoon I was watching a Billy Graham Crusade on television.   He was at the Anaheim Convention Center and they were singing that song, "Just as I Am" and when they came to the part that said, "Thy blood was shed for me," I cracked. God's Spirit fell on me like a ton of bricks. I started to sob uncontrollably. My wife came in from the kitchen to see what was wrong with me. All I could say was "I can't resist," "I can't resist." I kept saying it over and over again. I knew I would never be the same again after that. This was the beginning of my Christian life.

The next Sunday we went to the Billy Graham Crusade and I went forward with hundreds of other people. A counselor was there and he told me I should find a local church to join where I could learn the Scriptures so I could grow in Christ. Later on, I learned that this statement was not correct, but rather that I should grow in the knowledge of Christ.

At that time, my knowledge of the Bible was next to nothing. We finally joined a Baptist Church not far from our home. We attended it faithfully and eventually became very active. As teachers, I taught a junior class and my wife taught 4th grade. We were very dedicated and faithful. Later on, I became active in the bus ministry and my wife worked as a church secretary. Soon we were spending more time down at the church than we were at home. We were members of this church for about ten years.

Campus Crusade for Christ was very active in this church. The choir director was more or less the leader of this movement. The church had strong Pentecostal theology, but there was no speaking in tongues. The choir director held a class on how to live the victorious Christian life. I knew that I had some problems in my life with lust and anger, and I thought that maybe if I attended this class, I could overcome this problem. I attended the class for several weeks and did much studying of the Scripture, but I knew in my heart that I had not made any progress.

One evening after class, I took the teacher over to one side to explain to him my predicament. He looked me right in the eye and said, "Bob, I hate to tell you this, but you are possessed by the lust and anger demon."

This just about blew me away. I really did want to live the victorious Christian life. So I asked him, "What shall I do?"

He said "They will have to be driven out."

I thought, "Good grief. Is this going to hurt?" He made an appointment for me to go to another church. When I got there, I found out that I was not the only one with lust and anger thoughts. There was a whole room full of people there. One of the leaders gave us a short message and then the prayer time started. What happened next took me back to my childhood days when I went to the Pentecostal Church with my mother.

I have never heard so much wailing and screaming and damning the devil in all of my life. And then some men came over and put their hands on me and shook me. After much feverish prayer and damning the devil, we left. I knew in my heart that I had made a mistake going there. Did it help me? Of course not.

Later on I learned that we all have sinful thoughts. This is part of our Adamic nature. I understand now that these people were teaching "holiness doctrine" whereby obedience to the Scripture and by confession of sins, you can eradicate sin in your life. Sorry, but this didn't work. At least, it didn't work for me.

Later I learned that we are all sinners and that we all struggle with sin. Strength comes from knowing that God has dealt with our sin problem in the person of Jesus Christ. Because I was so active in this church, I became good friends with the pastor. His name was Doctor Lee. He liked to be called Doctor because he had a Doctorate in theology. He was a good friend and took an interest in me.

Every Saturday morning they had men's prayer meeting and Dr. Lee invited me to come. There were about seven or eight men attending and we would share our problems or the problems of other members and then we would get down on our knees and pray about these things. After that, we would go to a restaurant for breakfast.

I had many good Christian friends, but my best friend was Don. He was a Bible student and knew quite a bit about the Bible and had been a Christian for many years and was well grounded in the faith. We used to go out on visitation together to visit prospective church members or church members that were ill. Don did not have any Pentecostal tendencies nor was he an advocate of the holiness movement or Campus Crusade for Christ. He frequently told me that these people were immature Christians who really didn't know the truth about Christ or the Bible. I guess Don got me started thinking about what was true and what was false, what was right and what was wrong. I always knew there was something wrong in the church, but I couldn't put my finger on it.

After about five years of attending this church, I was nominated to become a deacon. I was pleased that someone had enough confidence in me to nominate me to be a deacon. There were already about 20 deacons, but I figured if they needed another one, I might as well be it. However, I heard through the grapevine that there might be a problem because I had been divorced. I spoke with Dr. Lee about this and told him that the divorce took place before I had become a Christian. He assured me that everything would be okay. The deacons had a special meeting to discuss this problem of my divorce and the possibility of me becoming a deacon. Dr. Lee was not prepared for what happened in that meeting.

There were more holiness deacons in that meeting than non holiness. The meeting lasted six hours. The holiness sited the scripture in 1st Timothy 3:12 that said a deacon should only have one wife. What the holiness Christians didn't know, was that it was customary for Jews to have two or three wives in those days. They voted on my becoming a deacon and I was denied. The pastor, Dr. Lee, was beside himself, as were a number of other deacons. I thought the church was going to split over this issue. However, it eventually died down and everybody forgot about this. My good friend Don said that the deacons had made a mistake because they didn't know the truth.

I continued to teach and work in the bus ministry, but I knew that Christ and what he had done for me had been offended. One Saturday morning during men's prayer meeting, Dr. Lee came in and he seemed very excited about something. He had some literature that he had read and said, "I'd like to give you men a copy of this literature. Please study it and tell me what you think about it."

I took it home and read it. It was written by a man from Australia named Robert Brinsmead. I learned later that Brinsmead was a Christian scholar and a lay theologian. The literature was very difficult for me to understand, because he was saying some things that I had never heard before and it didn't make sense to me.

One of the articles was about Peter on the day of Pentecost in Acts, Chapter 2. Brinsmead said in his article that the main thing here was the Gospel coming into the world and not the Holy Spirit, because in Acts 2, verse 11, they spoke about the wonderful works of God, which is the Gospel. This was my first breakthrough. I wanted to know more about this Gospel. I called Dr. Lee that evening to tell him what I had discovered. He confirmed what I had learned and said that there may be more for us to learn from Brinsmead. I wrote to Brinsmead and told him that if there were any future publications, I would like to receive them.

Dr. Lee preached a gospel, but it wasn't the same gospel that Brinsmead talked about. The gospel that Dr. Lee preached was that our sins were placed on Christ and God punished Christ on our behalf. And that was the extent of it. I was to learn later on that there was much more than that to it. As the months went by, I made it my priority to study whatever literature I could find and the Bible to find out what was the work of Christ, what had Christ really accomplished on our behalf. Dr. Lee was also studying this, and I think we both came into the knowledge that Christ was our representative before God and that God accepts the life, death and resurrection of Christ on our behalf.

This calls a lot of things into question. We discussed this frequently. I was anxious for Dr. Lee to preach this newfound doctrine to the congregation, but he never did. So one Sunday evening I went to his office, and knocked on the door. He invited me in. I sat across from him and said, "This church is void of the Gospel of Christ. When are you going to tell them that Christ has lived for them, died for them, rose again for them, and is God's right hand for them, and they are totally righteous and complete in him."

He looked at me for a while, then he got up, went over and closed the door, and came back and sat down. He looked at me again, leaned forward and said in a very low voice, "Bob, if I teach the Gospel in this church, they will run me off." I said, "What are you going to do." He said, "I don't know, but I know this, they will not accept the historical Gospel of Jesus Christ in this church."

I knew that Dr. Lee's days as a pastor there were numbered. He never did teach the Gospel. However, he did start making fun of their holiness doctrine.

One Sunday night while he was preaching to them, he said to them, "When you sin, who is doing the sinning? Is it the devil? Is it Jesus, or is it you?" Shortly after that, maybe a month or two, the deacons got together in a secret meeting and voted to fire Dr. Lee. He had been a pastor there for about ten years. I hated to see him go. Don and I became even closer after Dr. Lee left. I heard that he went down to Houston, Texas to another church, but it didn't work out for him there either.

I thought to myself after that happened, Jesus is still the rock of offense and a stumbling stone. The Gospel became even more meaningful to me after that, because I now understood that this was the Gospel that was taught by the Apostles. This was the Apostles' Doctrine, Acts 2:42. This is the Gospel that is offensive to holiness people who are religious. This is the Gospel that was responsible for the violent deaths of all the Apostles except for John.

After Dr. Lee left, I continued to teach there at the church, but the teaching was not well received. Sometimes three or four deacons would just pop in on my class to see what I was teaching. I had to be careful, because I was not ready to leave just yet.

My wife and I would invite friends over to our house for Bible study and teach them the Gospel there. We lost a lot of friends because of the Gospel. Some would even admit that this was what the Scripture says, but they loved being religious more than they loved the truth of the Gospel.

I was still receiving literature from Brinsmead and his literature was having somewhat of an impact on churches throughout the world. But because of the nature of the Gospel, it never really caught on. For one thing, he was a scholar, and he wrote for other scholars. Sometimes it was hard to understand what he was saying. We left that church and we tried other churches, but it was the same story all over again.

We even tried a Lutheran Church, we thought with their emphasis on justification by faith, that they would have correct doctrinal teaching. No such luck. I've been studying the Gospel for 30 years now, and I have found that the Gospel is not compatible with organized religion, nor is it compatible with a hierarchy. Many people hear the Gospel and say, "Yes, that's what I believe." The trouble starts when you show people that the Gospel calls into question many of their religious practices and beliefs.

The Apostle John wrote, *"Believe not every spirit, but try the spirits to see if they are of God."* 1st John 4:1. (KJV Mod.)

John 16:2 (KJV Mod.) *Jesus said, they shall put you out of the synagogues. Yes, the time is coming when those who murder you, will think they are doing service to God.*

The twelve apostles, and how they died:
    Andrew, was crucified.
    Bartholomew, was crucified.
    James, was beheaded.
    James, son of Alphaeus, was stoned to death.
    John, barely escaped a violent death.
    Judas, brother of James, was crucified.
    Matthew, was beheaded.
    Paul, was crucified.
    Peter, was crucified.
    Philip, was crucified.
    Simon, was crucified.
    Thomas, was thrust through with a spear.

Others, who were not of the twelve:
    Luke, was hanged.
    Mark, was dragged to death.
    Stephen, was stoned to death.
    Timothy, was beaten to death.

Romans 8:35-39 (KJV Mod) *Who or what shall separate us from the love of Christ, shall it be tribulation, distress, persecution, famine, nakedness, peril or sword. For the sake of Christ we die daily. We are accounted as sheep for slaughter.*
I am persuaded that neither death, life, angels, principalities, powers, things that are to come, height, depth, or any creature, shall be able to separate us from the love of God which is in Christ Jesus, our lord.

Jesus said, *"Come unto me all of you that labor and are heavy laden and I will give you rest. Take my yoke upon you and learn of me, for I am meek and lowly in heart and you shall find rest, rest for your souls, for my yoke is easy and my burden is light."* Matthew 11:28-30. (KJV Mod.).

This book is dedicated to all who will enter into His rest. *"There remains then a rest to the people of God."* Hebrews 4:9 (KJV Mod.).

Special thanks to Verdict Publications and all of the Christian Scholars that contributed to this enlightening magazine. You are the ones that inspired me to write this book.

Chapter 1
The Importance of Correct Doctrine

Doctrine, definition: "That which is presented for acceptance or belief; primarily signifies a principle that is taught; a theory as a preposition regarded as an acceptable verification, and thus is usually scientific. Any doctrine is a belief on the part of those who accept it, but belief more often suggests matters of faith rather than reason." *Funk and Wagnall's* Dictionary.

How important is doctrine in the Christian religion? It is very important to build our Christian faith upon correct doctrine. If we do not have correct doctrine, the Bible will not make sense and the Gospel message will not be properly understood. There are many doctrines, but there is only one doctrine concerning the Gospel message. It is the doctrine that was taught by the Apostles, especially the Apostle Paul.

The Gospel message is the heart of the Christian faith and when one comes to learn and understand the Gospel, it will be like a light that lightens the way. Many things that we think and do as Christians may be called into question by this marvelous light.

This book may be offensive to some. To some it may be a great joy. The Apostle Paul wrote in Romans 9:33 *"As it is written, behold, I lay in Zion a stumbling stone and a rock of offense."* (KJV Mod.) The stumbling stone is Christ. *"And whosoever believes in him should not be ashamed."*

The Apostles' Doctrine is not taught in most churches because of the freedom that it brings to the believer. Organized religion and the Gospel message simply are not compatible. I attended a Baptist Church for years and never really understood the Gospel message as it was taught by the Apostles. As a result of this, I was always in doubt of my salvation. Proper doctrine builds strong faith because the center of one's faith is turned to Christ, who is the focal point of the Gospel. Faith must go outside of itself. Religion turns faith into oneself, which is at its best very weak and full of flaws.

In Galatians 1:6-8, Paul wrote, *"I marvel that you are so soon removed from him that called you unto the grace of Christ unto another gospel, which is not another. But there be some that trouble you and would pervert the Gospel of Christ, but though we or an angel from heaven preach any other gospel unto you than that what we have preached unto you, let him be accursed."* (KJV Mod.)

This Scripture tells us that there is only one Gospel message and that there are some that would pervert it. The purpose of this book is to free you from religion. What is religion? Doesn't everyone have a religion?

The early Christians were fed to the lions and burned at the stake because they had no religion. All they had was faith in Christ. The Bible says that the first believers were called Christians. We need to go back to that period and try to see what they understood. The word religion basically means "mans effort to become acceptable to God by his own works or to please God by his actions or by what he has become.

The Apostles' Doctrine was not about religion. The word religion and law in most instances can be used interchangeably throughout the Bible. Religion, or law, says "do." The Gospel says, "done." Anything that tells you to do something is religion or law. The Gospel has freed us from religion and the law. We are now under grace. Paul wrote, *"For what the law or religion could not do in that it was a weak through the flesh, God sending his Son in the likeness of sinful flesh and for sin, condemned sin in the flesh."* Romans 8:3, (KJV Mod.) *"For Christ is the end of the law, or religion, for righteousness to everyone that believeth."* Romans 10:4. (KJV Mod.)

This is probably one of the most difficult things for Christians to understand is that they cannot please God by what they do. Only Christ was pleasing to God. The only thing that we can do to please God is to have faith in Christ.

Some Jews came to Jesus and said, "What shall we do that we might do the works of God?" Jesus said to them, *"This is the work of God, that you believe on him whom God has sent."* Matthew 6:28-29. (KJV Mod.)

Jesus never boasted about any work that any man had done, but he did say much about faith. It seems that in his ministry, he was seeking people that had faith. The poor widow who cast all that she had into the treasury, the Centurion soldier who asked Jesus to just say the word so his servant might be healed, the woman at the well who declared that Jesus was the Messiah, and many, many others. *"Without faith, it is impossible to please him."* Hebrews 11:6. (KJV Mod.)

The problem is, that all of our good works are tainted with pride and sin. Should this stop us from doing good works? Of course not. We should do good works out of gratitude for what Christ has done for us, but not for acceptance.

When Jesus was baptized, the voice from heaven said, *"This is my Son in whom I am well pleased."* Matthew 3:17 KJV Mod. No one has heard that since then. Perhaps we have all fallen short of what God expects from us. No, religion will not work. We must find another way. Having abandoned religion, we are now free to seek the Apostles' doctrine.

Paul said in 2nd Corinthians 4:3-4 (KJV Mod.), *"If our Gospel be hid, it is hid to them that are lost in whom the God of this world has blinded the minds of them which believe not. Lest the light of the glorious Gospel of Christ, who is the image of God, should shine onto them."*

I wish that I could teach you this Gospel, but you see, I really can't. Only the Holy Spirit can reveal it to you. If you read this book all the way through and still do not understand the Apostles' Doctrine, it's not my fault. You really didn't want to know it because you love being religious. This book will destroy your religion. If you don't want to be free from your religion, this book is not for you.

Chapter 2
The Gospel
and the Holy Spirit

The Gospel message came to the Apostles on the day of Pentecost (Acts, Chapter 2); it was accompanied by the Holy Spirit. The Holy Spirit is always present when the Gospel is presented. Some will have you believe that the Holy Spirit is the focal point here, but it is not. The Gospel is the main thing, not the Holy Spirit. The Holy Spirit does not speak of Himself, the Holy Spirit is given to draw attention to Christ and his Gospel.

Again, I must say that this demonstration of the Holy Spirit is about Christ and the Gospel. The men that spoke in tongues were speaking in a foreign language because there were men there that were from other countries and they heard the Gospel in their own language. (Acts 2:8).

What did they hear? They heard about the wonderful works of God, which is the Gospel. (Acts 2:11). The perversion takes place when well meaning, but misinformed Christians become hung up on the work of the Holy Spirit instead of the work of Christ. What was the result of the day of Pentecost? The Gospel and the Church were born.

Acts 2:42-44 says that they continued steadfastly in the Apostles' Doctrine and fellowship and in breaking of bread and in prayers and fear came upon every soul and many wonders and signs were done by the Apostles and all that believed, believed what? Believed the Gospel message were together and had all things common.

The Gospel unites. Religion divides. There are 79 religious denominations in the United States with over 150 different branches. This is the result of religion without a Gospel.

The day of Pentecost was a one-time event, never to be repeated again. The Lord gave birth to the Church with the Gospel message. The rest of the book of Acts is about the result of the Gospel message coming into the world. The message came with great power. The Apostles became bold in their preaching miracles occurred to authenticate that this message was from God.

Acts 5:42 says that the Apostles preached Christ every day and in every house and in the Temple. It doesn't say that they preached about how they experienced the wonderful sensation of receiving the Holy Spirit. As a matter of fact, very little is said about the Holy Spirit after the day of Pentecost, but much is said about Christ and his work for us.

The first Christian martyr was Stephen (Acts 7). After Stephen preached the Gospel to the Pharisees (Acts 7:57-59) says that they all ran upon Stephen and stoned him to death. The Gospel message is not a popular message. Please take note that Stephen presented the Gospel message in the background of the Old Testament. This is the way that the Apostles presented the Gospel. In the following chapters, we will see how the Old Testament is the framework for the Apostles' Doctrine.

Heresy is taught by placing something good in the place of what is the very best. The Holy Spirit is a good thing, but it is not what saves us. However, no one will be saved without the Holy Spirit. What saves us is Christ and his work for us. The Holy Spirit was the vehicle that God used to bring the Gospel message into the world. Jesus said, *"How be it when he, the Spirit of Truth has come, he will guide you into all Truth for he shall not speak of himself, but whatsoever he shall hear, that shall he speak, and he will show you things to come. He shall glorify me for he shall receive of me and shall show it unto you. All things that the Father has are mine. Therefore, he shall take of me and shall show it to you."* (John 16:13-15). (KJV Mod.)

Every time the Apostles were filled with the Holy Spirit, they spoke about Christ and his work for us. They spoke about the Gospel, Acts 2:14-40, Acts 7:55, Acts 8:29, Acts 10:44. The book of Acts is an account of the preaching of the Gospel in the power of the Holy Spirit. Please keep in mind that the New Testament had not yet been written. How else would God get the Gospel message out into the world on the day of Pentecost?

The Apostles were just common men. They had little, to no faith. Peter forsook Jesus along with the other Apostles. Thomas doubted Jesus' resurrection. But on the day of Pentecost, when the Gospel was revealed, they now knew what Christ had accomplished in his life, death and resurrection. They now knew what it was all about. Now they had a message, and it was a powerful one. The Apostles were transformed, and they were no longer weak fisherman and tax collectors. No, they were now powerful preachers of the Gospel. As a result of their boldness, they all died violent deaths except for the Apostle John. Read *Fox's Book of Martyrs*.

Today we have the full revelation of Jesus Christ and his work for us. We have a Bible. There is no need for full demonstrations of the Holy Spirit. No more signs and miracles. The full revelation of the Gospel is in the Bible. Signs and miracles would only take away from the importance of the Gospel. What is really more important, our experiences as Christians or Christ's experience in his living, doing, dying and resurrection?

What should be the Christian's focal point?   Spirit-filled Christians are Gospel-centered Christians. The Holy Spirit does not speak of himself, neither will one who possesses the Holy Spirit. The focus is always on Christ, and not on one's self. The Holy Spirit shows us for what we are and for what we will be. The Apostle Paul wrote, *"For we preach not ourselves, but Christ Jesus the Lord, and ourselves, your servants for Jesus sake. For God who commanded the light to shine out of the darkness has shined in our hearts to give the light of the knowledge, which is the Gospel of the glory of God in the face of Jesus Christ. But we have this treasure in earthen vessels that the excellency of the power of the Gospel may be of God and not of us.* 2nd Corinthians 4:5-8. (KJV Mod.)

The earthen vessels are our bodies. The treasure is the Gospel message. Earthen vessels are usually flawed and crack quite easily. Nevertheless, we possess the Holy Spirit within these earthen bodies for the purpose of bringing glory to God and Jesus Christ through the preaching of the Gospel message.   1st Corinthians 1:27-29 (KJV Mod.) says that *"God has chosen the weak things of the world to confound the things which are mighty and the things which are not, and things which are despised that no flesh should glory in his presence."*

This is why the Lord chose ordinary men to be his Apostles. He didn't choose the rich, well-educated Pharisees. He chose poor, uneducated fisherman, tax collectors, and the like. Today, most people want to go to a church that has money and a charismatic preacher. The religion of success is very popular throughout the country. I doubt if you will hear anything about Christ and his work in one of these churches. The Holy Spirit is the spirit of Christ. Christ became a life-giving spirit, 1st Corinthians 15:45. (KJV Mod.) *"And the Apostle further said the Lord is the Spirit."* 2nd Corinthians 3:17. (KJV Mod.)

We are at no disadvantage because we did not walk with Jesus. We now know him much better in a more intimate way. We have his spirit and the full revelation of him in the Bible. The spirit of Christ is in the world today. No church or institution has a monopoly on the Holy Spirit; not even Christianity. Wherever there is love, kindness, compassion, this is where the spirit of Christ is.

It is unfortunate that Christians get hung-up on what they think Jesus is doing or not doing in their lives. What really matters is what Jesus has done with our lives or with our souls. I'm sure none of us would exist today if it had not been for the saving work of Christ. I'm sure that if Jesus had failed in his mission of redemption, that God would have wrapped up this whole evil universe in one big ball of fire. But instead, we have heaven and eternal life through Christ, our Saviour and Lord. *"Eyes have not seen nor have ears heard, neither has it entered into the heart of man the things that God has prepared for them that love him. But God has revealed them unto us by his Spirit."* 1st Corinthians 2:9-10. (KJV Mod.)

How is a person born again? A man named Nicodemus came to Jesus with this question. The story is found in John, Chapter 3. Did Jesus tell Nicodemus to say a prayer? Did Jesus tell him to do anything at all? The answer is no. Jesus did say, *"as Moses lifted up the serpent in the wilderness, so must the Son of Man be lifted up."* Jesus was speaking of his crucifixion. *"That whosoever believeth in him (Christ) should not perish but will have eternal life. For God so loved the world that he gave his only begotten Son that whosoever believeth in him should not perish but would have everlasting life."* John 3:14-16 (KJV Mod.)

This is the first account of the Gospel in the New Testament spoken by Christ himself. We are born again by hearing the

Gospel and saying, "Yes, I want that." or "Yes, I need that." The message demands a response: accept or reject.

THE GOSPEL

God accepts the life, death and resurrection of Jesus Christ in our name and on our behalf. (See Hebrews 9:24 KJV Mod.)

Christ lived a life of perfect obedience to God's holy law. This life fulfilled the righteous demands of God's law for us and in our name and on our behalf. (See Romans 5:17-21 KJV Mod.).

In Christ's death on the cross, he satisfied the demand of God's holy law and removed us from the curse of a broken law and took our judgment in our name and on our behalf. (See Galatians 3:13 KJV Mod.)

In his resurrection, God fully accepts the life and death of Christ. The resurrection is God's stamp of approval on all that Christ has done for us and on our behalf. (see 1st Corinthians 15:14-22, KJV Mod.) We are justified and made complete in him. (See Colossians 2:10, KJV Mod.)

Christ is the new Adam or the new head, and representative of the human race. By his life, death and resurrection, he has offered to God all that is necessary for our salvation. We are saved by his work and not our own. (See Ephesians 2:8, KJV Mod.)

All who accept Jesus Christ and the work he has done for us are justified and saved by faith alone. We are saved by faith so that it may be by grace (God's goodness). Christ in heaven at God's right hand is our guarantee that our salvation is secure and certain. (See Hebrews 4:14-16, KJV Mod.)

Chapter 3
The Apostles' Doctrine and the Gospel

What is the Gospel? The Gospel concerns Jesus Christ, his life, death and his resurrection, his position at the right hand of God.

Then one may ask, "Who is Jesus Christ?" He is the new Adam. He is all that God can be and he is all that man can be. He is perfect God and perfect man in one person. He is the new head and representative of the human race. His father is God, his mother was human. He is the God-man.

John said, *"That which was from the beginning" which we have heard and we have seen him with our own eyes and with our hands, we touched him. This life was manifested and we saw it. This was the eternal life that was with the father."* 1st John 1:1-3 (KJV Mod.).

Jesus had to be all God and all man to save us. The first Adam failed because he was the head and representative of the human race; and we fell with him. We are all sons and daughters of Adam. He is our first father. We all have Adams' blood coursing through our veins. When Adam failed, the whole universe fell with him. We live in a fallen world and we are members of a fallen race.

Paul wrote, *"Wherefore as by one man, sin entered into the world and death, because of sin. So death passed upon all men because all are sinners."* Romans 5:12 (KJV Mod.). Many people don't like this. Some don't like to believe in original sin. All one has to do is turn on the evening news or pick up a newspaper to see that original sin is alive and well.

Paul again said, *"All have sinned and come short of the Glory of God."* Romans 3:23 (KJV Mod.). We are all sinners without works. What does this mean? It means that we didn't do anything to become a sinner. We are born this way. This is why we need to be born again. Peter wrote, *"being born again, not of corruptible seed, Adam, but of incorruptible Christ, by the word of God which lives forever."* 1st Peter 1:23. (KJV Mod.).

Just as we are sinners without works, so shall we become righteous without works. *"For as by one man's disobedience, many were made sinners; (Adam). So by the obedience of one, shall many be made righteous; (Christ.)"* Romans 5:19. (KJV Mod.).

If this is true, why is it that we are not righteous now? Because we still have Adam's blood coursing through our bodies. Even though we have the spirit of Jesus in our minds and in our hearts. This can cause a terrible struggle in one's life.

Paul said, *"The good that I would like to do, I don't do it; instead I do the evil. I really want to do good, but I do the evil."* He finally called himself a wretched man in Romans 7:15-24. (KJV Mod.). This is the problem of being a Christian sinner. Some would lead you to believe that you can get the victory over sin and become totally righteous. Unfortunately, this is not true. However, a complete understanding of the Gospel will give you considerable strength in your Christian life. This will take place, not because of something you do, but because of something you believe. This is why correct doctrine is so important.

The purpose of this book is to get your eyes off of your Christian life, which is tainted with sin, and get your eyes on the sinless Saviour. Once we know what has been accomplished on our behalf, we can say with Paul *"Let God be thanked that we were the servants of sin but we obeyed from our heart that form of doctrine which was delivered to us. Being then made free from sin, we became servants of righteousness."* Romans 6:17-18 (KJV Mod.).

There are loads of books on the market on how you can live the victorious life. All of these books have one thing in common: they all give you something to do and the focal point is usually yourself. The good news is that the victorious Christian life has already been lived and it was lived for you and on your behalf. It's the only life that God will accept.

THE LIFE OF CHRIST FOR THE BELIEVER

The question is, did Christ live for us as well as die for us? Most teachers of systematic theology will say, 'no.' They will say all that matters in the salvation of man is the death of Christ. His life is not relevant. My question is, what if Christ had failed to obey God's holy law? He would have been a transgressor and a sinner and his sacrifice on the cross would not have been acceptable to God. The law says *"We must love God with all of our heart, mind and strength and our neighbor as ourselves."* Leviticus 19:18 (KJV Mod.).

Was it necessary for Christ to fulfill this law for us? Yes. He fulfilled this law for us just as though we had fulfilled it ourselves. We are saved as much by his life as we are his death. The trouble with just accepting the death of Christ and not the life leaves a void in the believer's doctrine and either consciously or unconsciously the believer will try to fill this void with his own life. This is where the trouble starts.

This is why the focus of the believer will be on his life and not on the life of Christ. It was the life of Christ that offered perfect obedience to God. The voice from heaven said, *"This is my son in whom I am well pleased."* Matthew 3:17 (KJV. Mod.). Christ has provided righteousness for us by his life. The Scripture says *"For if by one man's offense, death reigned by one, but those who receive an abundance of grace and the gift of righteousness shall reign in one life by Jesus Christ."* Romans 5:17. (KJV Mod.).

Verse 19 says, *"For as by one man's disobedience, many were made sinners, so by the obedience of one shall many be made righteous."* The key word here is *made*. We are made righteous. It doesn't say we become righteous. This life of Christ is without spot or blemish. This is the life that offers everything to God that the law demands. This life that is perfect in word and in deed, this is our life; it is the life that God imputes to us. The Scripture says that Abraham believed that God was able to do that which he had promised and it was imputed to him for righteousness. Romans 4:21-22 (KJV Mod.).

This righteousness is the life of Christ, just as the sinful life of Adam was imputed to us, so will the righteous life of Christ be imputed to us. *"For as by one man's disobedience, many were made sinners, so by the obedience of one shall many be made righteous."* Romans 5:19 (KJV Mod.). *"For when we were enemies, we were reconciled to God by the death of his Son, much more being reconciled, we shall be saved by his life."* Romans 5:10 (KJV Mod.).

We need not only the life of Christ to save us, we need his death, his resurrection, his ascension into heaven, his presence at the right hand of God and his promise to come again and receive us unto himself. If we say that any part of this is not relevant, we have done great damage to the Gospel.

We must never lose sight of the fact that Christ is our representative before God and the new Adam. What he did in his life and death, he did for us. We need all of Christ to save us. God's holy law must be put to rest and a penalty must be paid for breaking the law. Christ has done this for us and on our behalf.

John wrote, *"Beloved, we are now the sons of God and it does not appear what we shall be, but we know when Christ appears, we shall be like him, for we shall see him as he is."* 1st John 3:2 KJV Mod. This is the final stage of sanctification. Our old Adamic nature will disappear in the twinkling of an eye and for the first time in our life we will be totally free from sin. Then we will experience the total righteousness of Christ, for all that he is and all that he has done will be ours. *"This is our inheritance, incorruptible and undefiled that will never fade away, reserved for us in heaven."* 1st Peter 1:4 (KJV Mod.). This is why Jesus said, *"Don't lay up for yourself treasure here on earth, but lay up for yourself treasure in heaven, for where your treasure is, there will your heart be also."* Matthew 6:19-21 (KJV Mod.).

The Gospel is essential to one's mental and physical well being. One reason that God hates sin is because of what it does to us. Look at what it did to Adam and Eve. The Scripture says that *"The way of the transgressor is hard."* Proverbs 13:15. (KJV Mod.).

Sin produces guilt and guilt produces all kinds of mental anxieties, to the point of even affecting your physical health. Many people turn to drugs and alcohol to get away from the burden of guilt. Guilt is a terrible burden to bear. The worse the sin, the worse the guilt. Some criminals have actually surrendered to the police because of the burden of guilt. Men are famous for confessing their adulterous affairs to their wives in the hope that they will no longer feel guilty.

Sometimes the guilt is worse than the sin. Self-punishment is common with people who have guilt and some have been known to commit suicide to escape their feelings of guilt. Others inflict themselves with all kinds of various methods to punish themselves thinking "I don't deserve anything good because I am bad." This usually results in more sin and more guilt.

Paul said, *"Because of God's law, the whole world stands guilty before God."* Romans 3:19. (KJV Mod.). That's why it is important for Christians to know that they are not under the law. It also is important for Christians to know that God has dealt with their sin in the person of Jesus Christ. No more sin problem means no more guilt problem. In God's eyes, we are as white as snow because of what Christ has done for us.

What does it matter what others think of us or what we might think of ourselves? What matters is what God thinks of us. Guilt is not always a bad thing, especially if it brings us to Christ. God's law is written on our heart and his Spirit comes to convict us of sin. It is a serious thing to resist the convicting power of the Spirit. If a person continues in sin and hardens their heart to the Spirit, after a while they will become reprobates and God gives up on them.

Paul wrote about some men who were homosexuals and did not want anything to do with God. He said God gave them up to be a reprobate mind (see Romans 1:28).

In India, millions plunge into the Ganja River once every 12 years to wash away their sins. This event is called Kumbh Mela Festival. This year they expect 65 million Hindus to participate. I have bad news for them. Wash as they may, they are still in their sins and they are still sinners. Only God can remove sin. A dip in the river will not do it. If you want your sins dealt with, you must come to Christ. Christ took our sins, past, present and future and buried them in Joseph's new tomb.

Gospel-believing Christians should not be studying the Scripture to see if they can figure out how they can get the victory over sin. In reality, if they do this, they are denying the fact that Christ has already done this for them. We are no longer in the sin fight. As Paul said, *"Now being made free from sin and having become servants to God, you have fruit into holiness and the end is everlasting life."* Romans 6:22 (KJV Mod.).

Do you really want to walk in the Spirit? Then read, study and believe the Gospel. I will guarantee that you will have great peace of mind in your heart, mind and spirit if you do this. Hebrews 4:10-11 (KJV Mod.) says that *"He that has entered into his rest (Christ's rest) has also ceased from his own works as God did from his."*

Jesus said, *"My yoke is easy, and my burden is light."* Matthew 11:30 (KJV Mod.). The Christian life is a life of rest. We don't have to do works to be acceptable anymore. Christ has done the work for us in our name and on our behalf. Christ is our new humanity. When he lived, we lived in him. When he died, we died with him. When he arose, we arose with him. We lived, died and arose from the dead in him. If you can understand this and all that it calls into question, you are now a theologian. This is the Gospel that was taught by the Apostles.

How do we know that our salvation is assured? Because God accepted all that Jesus did and we were accepted in him. Our salvation is secure in heaven because Jesus is at God's right hand. (see Hebrews 12:2, (KJV Mod.). Colossians 2:10 says, *"We are complete in him."* Paul wrote, *"If we are now risen with Christ, we should seek those things which are above where Christ is at the right hand of God. Set your affections or heart on things above, not on earthly things, for we are dead and our life is hid with Christ. When Christ appears, who is our life? Then shall we appear with him in Glory."* Colossians 3:1-4. (KJV Mod.).

Do you want the higher Christian life? This is where it's at. God has placed our salvation in a very secure and safe place. No one can steal it, no one can corrupt it. Jesus said, *"Don't lay up treasure on earth where moth and rust can corrupt and where thieves break through and steal, but lay up for yourselves treasure in heaven."* Matthew 6:19-21 (KJV Mod.).

"Jesus is the pearl of great price, that when a man finds it, he sells all that he has to own it." Matthew 13:45-46 (KJV Mod.). Is Jesus yours? Have you accepted his salvation? Or do you have your own do-it-yourself salvation?

The Scripture says that there is a way that seems right to a man, but the end of it is damnation. The way that seems right is religion.

Trying to go to heaven by being good. No matter how many good things we do, it will not buy us heaven. As the Scripture says, *"For by Grace, (God's goodness), are you saved, by faith and not that of yourself. It is the gift of God."* Ephesians 2:8 (KJV Mod.).

Jesus said *"Many will say unto me in that day 'Lord, Lord. Have we not preached in your name? And in your name cast out devils and in your name have we not done many wonderful works?' and Jesus said, "Depart from me, you who work iniquity. I never knew you."* Matthew 7:21-23 (KJV Mod.).

No, religion is not the answer. Accept the fact that you are a sinner and in desperate need of being saved, and let Jesus do the saving.

Chapter 4
The Apostles' Doctrine and the Resurrection

The resurrection was the main emphasis of the Apostles' teaching. Paul said, *"If there is no resurrection of the dead and Christ is not risen, then our preaching is in vain. So also is your faith."* 1st Corinthians 15:13-14 (KJV Mod.).

Much theology today starts with the cross, but it is really the resurrection that is the main thrust of the Apostles' doctrine. Systematic theology emphasizes the cross for salvation. That may be true, but not completely. When Christ died on the cross, it was the fulfillment of the law. Christ bore the curse of the broken law in his own body. The human race was crucified in him. The law says that the soul that sins must die. Christ took our death for us. When he died, the whole human race died with him. (See Romans 6:3-7 (KJV Mod.).

Some would have you believe that God imputed the sins of humanity on Christ and then punished Christ as a sinner. In other words, Christ paid for our sins. This is not correct doctrine, because it appears that God must have his pound of flesh before he can forgive sins. Not only that, it is very legalistic. Payment and satisfaction are legal terms. Romans 6:8 (KJV Mod.) says that *"If we be dead with Christ, we believe we shall also live with him."* God put to death the Adamic race in Christ. When he died, we died with him.

When Christ was resurrected, the whole human race was resurrected with him, spiritually speaking. See 1st Corinthians 15:21-22

(KJV Mod.): *"For since by man came death, (Adam), by man came also the resurrection, (Christ). For as in Adam, all die, so in Christ, shall all be made alive."* The resurrection of the saints is yet to come, but Christ has paved the way for us because he lives, we shall live also.

The resurrection is not going to be good for everyone. Jesus said, *"Marvel not at this for the hour is coming when all that are in the graves shall hear his voice and shall come forth. They that have done good unto the resurrection of life and they that have done evil unto the resurrection of damnation."* John 5:28-29 (KJV Mod.).

The Apostles believed in a final judgment. Not only of those outside of Christ, but also of those in Christ. Paul said, *"We shall all stand before the judgment seat of Christ and every knee will bow and every tongue confess so then everyone will give account of himself to Christ. But there shall be no condemnation for those who are in Christ."* John 5:24 (KJV Mod.).

The resurrection of Jesus was God's stamp of approval on all that Christ had done in his life and death and resurrection. If Christ had failed to live up to God's expectation, there would not have been a resurrection, and we would have been without hope. Before the resurrection, all was doom and gloom for the Apostles. The resurrection turned the world upside down. There is no greater event in human history than the resurrection of Jesus Christ. Paul wrote to Timothy: *"Remember Jesus Christ raised from the dead, this is my Gospel."* 2nd Timothy 2:8 (KJV Mod.).

What if the story of Jesus ended at the cross? There is no hope in a dead Christ. There is no saving work in the Holy Spirit as most Catholics would have you believe. The Holy Spirit does not make us holy. Christ makes us holy by what he has done on our behalf.

The resurrection is the foundation of the Christian faith. It means that all that Christ did and claimed to be was true. He is either who he claimed to be or he is a fraud. If Jesus was a fraud, then he is still buried in Joseph's new tomb. If he is the Lord of Lords and the King of Kings, the one who defeated the devil, abolished death, put away sin, established righteousness, fulfilled the law, opened the gates of heaven and saved the human race, let's give him his rightful place as Lord, which is at the right hand of God.

The resurrection means that death is not the end, but is only the beginning. This life that we live now is the seed life. It's the life that goes into the ground. We cannot experience eternal life unless we die. As Paul said, *"As we have born the image of the earthly. So shall we also bear the image of the heavenly."* 1st Corinthians 15:49 (KJV Mod.). We look forward to a new life, a new body, a new hope. We look for a new city where Christ will reign in righteousness. In the meantime, we will have to get through this life the best that we can.

There are no physical benefits to being a Christian, as some would have you believe. The rain falls on the just and the unjust. There are just as many Christians dying of cancer as there are atheists. But we have this hope, as Paul said, *"I reckon that the sufferings of this present time are not worthy to be compared with the glory which shall be revealed in us."* Romans 8:18 (KJV Mod.).

So hang in there, friend. This life is only temporary. The next life is eternal.

Chapter 5
The Apostles' Doctrine and the Christian Life

Christianity is an objective religion. That is, it goes outside of itself. The focal point is always Jesus Christ outside of us and what he has accomplished on our behalf. This was always the thrust of the Apostles' doctrine. To internalize Jesus Christ will lead to a life of doubt and mysticism.

The big question in most religious circles is what is Jesus doing in your life? Or some might ask, are you living the Spirit-filled life? I always have trouble with these kinds of questions because they are subjective. As far as I know, God is finished with the human race. Why would anyone want to bring Jesus down and into their life?

I think we should leave Christ in heaven and not back into the dregs of society. The Scripture says nothing about Jesus living his life through us. Why would he want to do this? He is pure and without sin. No, let's leave Jesus in heaven.

There is a spirit-filled life. Remember the Holy Spirit does not speak of himself, but instead glorifies Christ. A spirit-filled Christian will want to talk about Christ, his life, his death and his resurrection, not about himself or how he got the victory of some little itty-bitty sin in his life. Frankly, this is a real turn off for me. I would rather not hear about some mystical religious experience that someone has had that degrades Christ and his work for us.

The Scripture says, *"In these last days, God has spoken to us by his Son. And after purging our sins, He has sat down at the right hand of God."* Hebrews 1:2-3 (KJV Mod.). God has said all that he is going to say to the human race when he gave us Christ. The full revelation of God is in Christ. Not only that we have a complete Bible. But I know that some want a personal word from the Lord. Sorry, there isn't one; only the one that you manufacture in your head. I know that this is not popular to speak this way, but lets be truthful and bring glory to Jesus. That should be our purpose in life.

When the Apostles exhorted others to live a better life or to turn from sin, it was always because of what Christ had done for them. Paul said, "*I beseech you brethren, by or because of the mercy of God that you present your bodies as a living sacrifice, holy and acceptable to God, which is your reasonable service.*" Romans 12:1, KJV Mod.).

This is something for us to do. Why should we do this? Because God is merciful in sending Jesus into the world to save us from sin. We live the Christian life out of gratitude for what Christ has done for us. We don't live the Christian life to become accept- able. We are already accepted in Christ. He is our representative. The only life that is pleasing to God is the life of Christ.

Antichrist puts something good in the place of what is best. The Christian life is good and everyone who has faith in Christ should live it to the utmost.

I have been accused of being a liberal Christian. Perhaps I am. I drink a little wine occasionally and if there is a good movie, I may go see that. But I'm not bound by any religious creeds or dogma. The Christian life should be a life of freedom. The Gospel allows us to be human. Religion wants you to be like God.

The Bible is not necessarily about the Christian life, which is a good thing. The Bible is about Jesus Christ, which is the best thing. The focal point should always be Jesus Christ and his work for us. If the Christian life becomes a focal point, we have put the cart before the horse.

The motivating force in the Apostles' lives was Jesus Christ and him crucified and risen. (See 1st Corinthians 2:2). Most of the thinking in the churches today is now that you are saved, we are going to teach you how to be a strong Christian witness for Christ, and in doing this, they literally throw out the baby with the water. The new convert will become bombarded with Scripture that tells him what to do (which is law).

Christians should not be motivated by law, but by grace. The Pharisees were motivated by law. The goodness of God and the Gospel should always be the motivating power in a Christian's life. The Gospel calls for a response. How can one hear that the Son of God left heaven and came to this earth to die on a wooden cross for the sake of saving a bunch of rebellious sinners and not respond to it? Or worse yet, reject it? This is a mystery to me.

Paul wrote, *"How shall we escape if we neglect such great salvation?"* The answer is, we won't. The Scripture says, *"It is appointed unto man to die and after that, the judgment."* Hebrews 9:27 (KJV Mod.).

Other Scripture says *"It is a fearful thing to fall into the hands of the living God."* Hebrews 10:31 (KJV Mod.). I can't imagine what it would be like to stand before God in the judgment without Christ. In the judgment, if you are a Christian, God will not see you at all. He will only see Jesus Christ. How wonderful that will be!

We really don't want to see God when we are in these sinful bodies, but we will be changed because of Christ and we will then be fit for heaven. *"So when this corruptible shall put on incorruption and this mortal shall have put on immortality this shall be brought to pass the saying that it is written that death is swallowed up in victory, or death where is your sting? O grave, where is your victory? But thanks be to God who gives us a victory through our Lord, Jesus Christ. Therefore, my brothers, be steadfast and unmovable. Always abounding in the work of the Lord."* 1st Corinthians 15:54-58 (KJV Mod.).

The greatest Christian that ever lived was the Apostle Paul. Before his conversion, he was a Pharisee and a persecutor of Christians. He was responsible for the deaths of many Christians. He was there when Stephen was stoned to death. (See Philippians 3:6).

Paul said that he persecuted the church with zeal. After his traumatic conversion to Christ on the road to Damascus, Paul became the most dedicated Christian the world has ever known. He was the only Pharisee called by Christ to become an Apostle.

Many of the books of the New Testament were written by Paul. Much of the doctrine taught by the Apostles was written by Paul. Paul was the first one to take the Gospel to the gentiles. Most of the doctrine of the Gospel can be found in the book of Romans, chapters 5 and 6. This was written by Paul. I suppose if a person needed a model for a Christian, Paul would be the ideal.

According to *Fox's Book of Martyrs*, Paul was beheaded in Rome under the reign of Nero. Before his death, he wrote, *"For I am now ready to be offered and the time of my departure is at hand. I have fought a good fight, I have finished my course. I have kept the faith. Henceforth, there is laid up for me a crown of righteousness which the Lord shall give me at that day and not to me only, but to them also who love his appearing."* 2nd Timothy 4:6-8 (KJV Mod.).

Chapter 6
The Apostles' Doctrine and the Life of Freedom

Jesus said, *"If the Son shall make you free, you shall be free, indeed."* John 8:36 (KJV Mod.). What did Jesus mean by this? Paul wrote, *"For the law of the Spirit of life in Jesus Christ has made me free from the law of sin and death. For what the law or religion could not do in that it was weak through the flesh, God sending his Son in the likeness of sinful flesh and for sin condemned sin in the flesh."* (Romans 8:2-3, KJV Mod.).

Christ destroyed sin and religion. Religion is the sin of the flesh. All religious people have one thing in common: they are all proud of their religion. "Better not say anything about Baptists or Methodists, or whatever. Don't question the preacher or the creeds or doctrines of the church, just sit there and shut up or you will be labeled a troublemaker." Jesus said he didn't come to send peace on earth, but a sword. (Matthew 10:34).

If you are going to be a Gospel-centered Christian, you had better expect trouble from the religious people. Remember it was the religious people that had Christ put to death. It was not the sinners that gave Jesus a bad time, it was the religious Torah packing Pharisees that harassed him every where he went. They had their scriptures and the law and they used both to condemn Jesus to death. Beware of religious men.

Religion is like living in a box. You know exactly where the walls are and the ceiling and the floor are. You can be very comfortable in the box and you can feel very secure. Religion is fine as long as no one jostles your box.

The resurrection doctrine turns the religious box upside down and those inside may not like it because of the freedom that it brings. The Gospel message says, "Hey, you don't have to live in the box anymore. Come outside where the air is fresh and you can move around." But they may reply, "No, we don't feel secure or safe outside of our box. It's scary out there."

The Gospel brings total freedom because our salvation is not based on how well you perform, but rather on how well Christ has performed. That's what Jesus meant when he said, "If the Son shall make you free, you shall be free, indeed."

If we are going to be a witness for Christ, we must have freedom. We can't go live in a monastery and be a witness for Christ. Jesus said to go into all the world and preach the Gospel. We must have the freedom to associate with people of every kind regardless of who they are or what they believe. We must have the freedom to go into any place, regardless of where it might be.

Paul said, *"I can become all things to all men that I might win some."* 1st Corinthians 9:22 (KJV Mod.). Jesus ate and drank with sinners. The Pharisees accused him of being a wine bibber and a friend of sinners (see Matthew 11:19, KJV Mod.). Peter was eating with the Gentiles when some Jews showed up. Peter apparently went under the table, because according to Jewish law, you don't eat with Gentiles, because it's a sin.

When Paul saw they were not living according to the Gospel, he said to Peter, "Are you going to be a Jew or a Gentile? Don't compel the Gentiles to be like Jews. We must have the freedom to be all things to all men." Peter did the wrong thing and Paul rebuked him because it was not according to the Gospel (see Galatians 2:11-15, KJV Mod.).

Religious people cannot go into the world. They are too busy with their religious baggage. They must have their church and all the religious paraphernalia that goes with it. The Gospel allows us to be free and human. Religion tries to make us like God.

The problems in the world today are the result of religion. Religion fills the void where there is no Gospel or a subverted Gospel. Christians are called to live by faith in Christ. Those outside of Christ live by law or religion. Paul wrote, *"Knowing that a man is not justified by the works of the law or religion, but by faith in Jesus Christ. Even we who have believed in Jesus Christ that we might be justified by faith and not by works of the law or religion. For by the works of the law or religion, shall no flesh be justified."* Galatians 2:16 (KJV Mod.).

There is no freedom in religion. There are only laws upon laws, rules upon rules, creeds upon creeds, do, do, do. The Jews took the Ten Commandments and came up with six hundred and thirty rules for living. On the Sabbath Day, you are not allowed to turn off a light or flush a toilet. This is called being in bondage to the law. Paul had a problem with the Galatians. They kept wanting to bring in their Jewish religion and mix it with Christianity and pervert the Gospel. (See Galatians 1:6-7).

Paul, being frustrated, said, *"O foolish Galatians. Who tricked you that you should not obey the truth. Before whose eyes Jesus Christ was publicly crucified. This only thing I want to find out from you. Did you receive the Spirit by the works of the law, or by being religious? Or by hearing the Gospel?"* Galatians 3:1-2 (KJV Mod.).

Judaism is the father of a religion. Catholicism is the mother of it. All religions regardless of what they are stem from these two religions. From these two religions will come the Antichrist spoken of in Revelation 13:11-18. Multitudes will be deceived because they do not understand the Gospel or don't want it.

Religion is the natural way. It appears to be the most logical thing to do. You try to lead a good life, go to church, read the Bible, try not to offend anyone, do good works, be kind to animals, don't cheat, steal or lie, and one might think surely God will recognize what a good person I am and take me to heaven. Wrong!

Keep in mind that was God's Son hanging on the cross for you. If you think you can skirt around that or deny it, you are in danger of hell fire. Jesus said, *"Enter in at the straight gate, for wide is the gate and broad is the way that leads to destruction, and many there be that go that way. Because straight is the gate and narrow is the way that leads to life and few there be that find it."* Matthew 7:13-14 (KJV Mod.).

Religion is the broad way. Jesus is the narrow way. Does this mean that since we are saved by Grace through faith apart from works, we can live as we please? Paul wrote, *"Don't let sin reign in your bodies that you should obey the lust of it. Rather yield yourselves unto God for sin shall not have dominion over you for you are not under the law but under Grace."* Romans 6:12-14 (KJV Mod.).

This Scripture is law because it tells us to do something. However, we must look at the motivating factor. Are we to do this to please God? No. That would be religion. We do this because we are under Grace. Grace did not come cheap. Christ hanging on the cross on our behalf is not cheap Grace. Another reason is that because of the Gospel, we believe that our sins have been dealt with. If Christ has abolished sin, we should live like it.

There is no power in religion because it is all based on your performance. People are always asking, "Have you committed your life to Christ? Have you been born again? Have you been baptized? What church do you attend? These are all questions to see how religious you are so they can judge you.

When someone starts asking questions, I just tell them, "I'm just another sinner saved by Grace" and that is usually the end of the probing. It also means that I'm not a hypocrite. I've already confessed that I'm a sinner. That means that I might be capable of almost anything. Religious people don't like to think of themselves as sinners. The worst kinds of sinners are religious sinners. Those are the kind that can kill you in the name of God and think they are doing a service to God by getting rid of you. Ask any Protestant or Catholic in Ireland.

The Gospel allows us to be truly human. It's okay if you fail once in a while. That just proves that you are a member of the human race. When is the last time somebody told you it's okay to screw up? Paul said that he was the chief of all sinners (1st Timothy 1:15 (KJV Mod.). Where does that leave you and me?

Accept your sinnerhood and go on living. Get your eyes off of your inadequacies and get your eyes on the all sufficient Christ.

Chapter 7
The Apostles' Doctrine and the Bible

I've often wondered how much different the world and history would be if we did not have the Bible. The early Christians did not have a Bible. The only ones that had access to Old Testament Scriptures were the Jewish Pharisees. Word about Christ was communicated orally or by letters from Paul, but mainly by word of mouth.

The Gentile Christians were more easily converted to Christianity than the Jews because they did not have a religion, but they did worship false gods. The Apostles usually preached the Gospel in the framework of the Old Testament. The Gospel outside of the Old Testament does not make sense. The Old Testament reveals the failure of man right back to Adam, who is the father of the human race.

In Stephen's sermon to the Pharisees, he rehearsed the failure of Israel to obey God. He finally ended the sermon by telling them that they were stiff-necked and uncircumcised of their heart and were murderers of the prophets. The Scripture says that when they heard these things, they were cut to the heart and they gnashed their teeth and stopped their ears. Then they drug Stephen out of the city and stoned him to death. (See Acts, Chapter 7).

The Jews always did their dirty work outside of the walls of Jerusalem because they thought their city was holy. Christ was crucified outside of the city. The Old Testament is about God bringing forth a people from whom the Saviour of the world would come. Somehow the Jews missed that, even though the Old Testament is full of prophecies about the coming of the Messiah.

There are also many symbols and types in the Jewish religion that portrays Christ as the Messiah. The most remarkable picture of Christ is found in Isaiah Chapter 53. Why didn't the Jews see the coming of their Messiah? They got hung up on the Ten Commandments or the law. The purpose of the law was to preserve the Jewish nation, that is, to hold it in tact until Christ came. Without the law, there probably would have been another Sodom and Gomorrah and that possibly would have subverted the genetic line from which Christ would have come. (See Matthew Chapter One).

The Pharisees rejected Christ because he did not fit into their religious mold. Their Messiah would never eat and drink with sinners, nor would he touch lepers or fellowship with what they thought was the scum of the earth. No, he would come to the Temple and teach them great things about the law and the Pharisees would rule and reign with Christ. This is what they thought.

The Pharisees were blinded by their traditions and their religion. When Christ began to do miracles, they went into denial. Is this not the Son of Joseph, the carpenter? They said, how can this be the Messiah? So they followed him around Jerusalem trying to trap him in his teachings. But it didn't work and the Pharisees became even more frustrated with Christ, especially when the multitudes went after him.

Finally the Jews became so frustrated that they devised a plan to murder him. It was after the raising of Lazarus. They said the whole world was going after him (John 12:19). So the die was cast. The Jewish religion was about to collapse. The Pharisees had become the laughing stock of Jerusalem. (See John 12:42).

Religion is indeed a dangerous thing. Even though the Old Testament speaks of Christ and his coming, the Jews missed it. I wonder if the Church will miss the Second Coming? Christians are so pre-occupied with their Christian lives, I don't think they are looking for him to come again. If he did come, I doubt if they would be happy about it.

I don't know what the church will do in heaven. There is no religion in heaven. No church to go to, no Bible study. What will they do? Maybe they won't be happy there.

We should keep in mind, the Bible was written by Jewish men who were under the law. As a matter of fact, most of the Bible was written under the law. The only one who really understood the Apostles' doctrine was the Apostle Paul. The rest of them had a combination of Jewish religion and Christianity. This was the problem in the early church and it's the same problem that exists today. Law and Grace simply will not mix. As a result of this, most Christians are confused about how they are saved, nor do they know how to interpret the Scriptures.

Paul had this problem with the Galatians. They heard the Gospel and believed it, but they wanted to mix it up with the Jewish religion. So Paul tried to bring them back to the Gospel (Galatians Chapter 3:4-5). We should keep in mind that Paul's letters were directed to Christians that wanted to bring the law or the Jewish religion into their Christian theology and that Paul's letters were always in defense of the Gospel.

If we read Paul's letters carefully, we can see the stress that Paul injected into his letters, and at times, his frustration. It is apparent that the Jewish Christians who still held on to the law were following Paul around, trying to undo his doctrine of Grace with their doctrine of Grace and law. It is unfortunate that the Gospel is offense to some. It seems that man is just not happy unless he is participating in his own salvation by being religious.

Pride will probably be responsible for taking multitudes to hell. To be saved, you must acknowledge that you have a sin problem and you need Christ to be saved from the consequences of sin. Religion, or the law, is our schoolmaster to lead us to Christ. Paul wrote, *"We are all under sin, that the promise of faith in Jesus Christ might be given to them that believe. The law was our schoolmaster to bring us to Christ that we might be justified by faith. But after faith has come, we are no longer under the schoolmaster, because we are all children of God by faith in Jesus Christ."* Galatians 3:22-26 (KJV Mod.).

The Bible was given to us to reveal Jesus Christ and his work for us. If the Bible is used for any other purpose than this, the Gospel message is subverted. The Bible is not for instruction in Christian living as some would have you believe, nor is it a book on how you can please God. Again, I must say, that the Bible was written to reveal Jesus Christ and what he has accomplished on our behalf. If you are studying the Bible to learn more about Christ, then the Holy Spirit will be there to enlighten you and show you things too marvelous to comprehend (2nd Peter 1:1-4, KJV Mod.).

Jesus is the word of God (John 1:1, (KJV Mod.). He is the living word of God. He is the word that became flesh and dwelt among us. John said, *"We touched him and beheld his glory as of the only begotten of the Father, full of Grace and Truth."* John 1:14 (KJV Mod.).

Every prayer that we have ever prayed was answered when God gave us Christ. The only part of the Bible that can be considered to be the Word of God is the part that reveals Christ and his work for us. The Bible can be divided into two parts: the part that says 'do' which is law, and the part that says, 'done,' which is Gospel. It is important for us not to mix up these two aspects up of the Bible or we will have confusion.

It is not uncommon for Christians to take scripture about what Christ has done for us and turn it into something for them to do. Example: 2nd Corinthians 5:17 (KJV Mod.) says, *"That if any man be in Christ, he is a new creation or creature."* This is not something we do, this is about something Christ has done for us. Jesus is the new creation and because we are in him, we are new creations. We had nothing to do with this (Colossians 1:15-21, KJV Mod.). However, we should act like new creations. (Colossians 3:1-4, KJV Mod.).

The Christian life is always lived because of what Christ has done for us. Paul says, *"If you are risen with Christ, then seek those things which are above."* We are called to act out what has been accomplished for us. This is the Christian life. Play your position in Christ.

Should we be concerned about sin? No, because our position in Christ is that we were crucified with Christ, that the body of sin might be destroyed so we don't have to be in bondage to sin (Romans 6:6-7, KJV Mod.). We have been made righteous and we should act like it. Even though we know we are not, but we yield ourselves to righteousness. We turn from sin to righteousness because this is our position in Christ (Romans 6:16-18, (KJV Mod.). This is called living in the Spirit.

Paul wrote, *"For the law of the Spirit of life in Jesus Christ has made me free from the law of sin and death."* Romans 8:1-5 (KJV Mod.). This is called "living in the Gospel." Many Christians seem to think that these verses are something for them to do. Example Galatians 2:20 (KJV Mod.), Paul says, *"I'm crucified with Christ, never the less, I live, yet not I, but Christ lives in me."* We cannot crucify ourselves so that we can have more of Christ in us no matter what you do, either physically or mentally.

Again, this is not something for us to do, but something that Christ did for us. It is heresy to internalize these Scriptures and those that do this do great harm to the Gospel and are Antichrist.

The holiness movement started in the early 1900's under the under the name of Pentecostalism. Again, it is a mixture of Judaism and Christianity with a dose of Catholicism. Most of the Gospel Scripture was internalized. This movement infiltrated all of the Protestant churches in most circles and is still alive and well. The Catholic part of Pentecostalism was miracles and mysticism; this being mixed with Judaism and keeping the law made for one pretty screwed up Christian, if they are Christians.

One doesn't have to go very far to find a Pentecostal. They are in every church talking about the wonderful experience of being filled with the Holy Spirit, of which they may not have. Scripture says, that the Holy Spirit does not speak of himself. It is not correct doctrine to mix up the work of Christ and the work of the Spirit. The work of Christ is a finished work.

As Jesus said before he died on the cross, "It is finished." He is now in heaven at the right hand of God as our intercessor. The Spirit's work is within the believer. Christ's work is outside of us. The Spirit convinces us of sin and draws us to Christ and glorifies Christ. We cannot say that the Spirit died on the cross or that the Father ascended into heaven. We know that this would be grave error, nor should we mix up the person of Christ with the Spirit. The work was different. It's best to keep them separate.

The Holy Spirit is the driving force of the Gospel. It is also the motivating force of the Gospel. As Paul said, *"For our Gospel came to you not only in word, but also in power and in the Holy Spirit."* 1st Thessalonians 1:5 (KJV Mod.).

The word was the Gospel. In the New Testament, the word of God is usually referring to Christ. To most Christians, the Bible is the Torah for Christian living. Just as the Jews used the Old Testament for religious living. There is very little difference between the two. They are both living by law and not by spirit. Nowhere in the Bible does Jesus instruct the disciples to study Old Testament Scripture for holy living. But he did direct them to Scripture that testified of him. This was a radical breakthrough for the disciples.

Old Testament Scripture was to be used as a witness to Christ and not for holy living or obedience to God. The New Testament is to be used in the same way: as a witness to Christ. John wrote, *"These things are written that you might believe that Jesus is the Christ, the Son of God, and that believing, you may have life in his name."* John 20:31 (KJV Mod.).

If the Bible is used for any other purpose than to reveal Christ, it is a subversion of the Gospel. Jesus said to the Pharisees, *"You study the Scriptures, for in them you think you will find eternal life."* John 5:39 (KJV Mod.).

Acts 17, Paul is in a synagogue with some Jews and he is reasoning with them out of the Old Testament scripture concerning the Gospel of Christ. Some believed and some didn't. Verse 11 says that they studied the scriptures daily to see if those things that Paul had declared were true. Bible study is fine, as long as you are studying to see if the doctrine the Apostles preached is true and all the things that Christ claimed to be are true. Is the Gospel message true? Read the Bible for yourself to see if these things are true.

Anyone can understand the Bible if it is read in the light of the Gospel. The Gospel is the guiding light. All things must be judged in the light of the Gospel, even the Bible itself. If it is not according to grace, mercy and the Gospel of Christ, disregard it. If you are going to study the Bible so as to increase your knowledge of what is right or what is wrong, welcome to the school of Pharisaism.

No documents or letters were ever written by Jesus. Jesus didn't teach out of the Old Testament like the Scribes and Pharisees did. Nor did Jesus instruct anyone to record his life, death and resurrection. Perhaps there was something here that was just too big to be recorded on paper.

John said that Jesus did so many things that the world would not be big enough to hold the books that could be written about it (John 2:25, (KJV Mod.). What John was really saying was that this is so great, it's not describable. It's so big, that it's mind-boggling. Peter said it is so great that it is unspeakable (see 1st Peter 1:8).

Does the Bible do justice to Christ? Of course not. We only have a rough sketch of what he is really like. The Apostles tried to convey his person in writing, but you see, it is just not possible to do that. However, we know enough about him to trust him as Lord and Saviour.

John wrote, "*These things are written that you might believe that Jesus is the Christ, the Son of God, and that believing, you might have life in his name.*" John 20:31 (KJV Mod.). There is only one Jesus and we know enough about him that we will not be deceived by false Christ's. There is one Jesus, one Spirit, one Gospel. It is our responsibility to recognize them, identify them, and know what is true. No one can do this for you. Read the Bible yourself so that you are not deceived.

Paul wrote, *"The time is coming when they will not endure sound doctrine, but after their own lust, shall they go after teachers who having itching ears and they shall turn away from the truth and will turn to fables."* 1st Timothy 4:3-4 (KJV Mod.).

John wrote, *"Believe not every spirit, but try the spirits to see if they are of God, because many false prophets are gone out into the world."* 1st John 4:1 (KJV Mod.). Everything should be tried in the light of the Gospel. If it isn't according to the Gospel, disregard it.

It's very easy to be deceived when you are seeking the truth. I've been deceived more times than I can remember. Sometimes a preacher will say things that seem like truth, but you must listen carefully. If it is not true, it will usually become confusing, because they are mixing grace and law.

Bishop Pollock says, "The Bible is a corridor between two eternities down which walks the Christ of God. His invisible steps echo through the Old Testament, but we meet him face to face in the throne room of the new. It is through that Christ alone, crucified for me, that I have found forgiveness of sins and eternal life. The Old Testament is summed up in a word: Christ. The New Testament is summed up in the word: Jesus. And the summary of the whole Bible is that Jesus is the Christ."

Is the Bible infallible? Of course it is. The Bible was written by men; sinful men. The Holy Spirit does not do a perfect work through humans. Even though men were inspired by the Spirit to write, the human element was present in the writings.

Again, I must say that the purpose of the Bible is to reveal Jesus Christ and his work for us. The Bible is not holy nor is it sacred. It is not a guide to live by. That was never the intention of the writers to give us a book to live by. Much of the Bible condones slavery. Even the Apostle Paul said that the women should not speak in the church. If you were to live by the Bible, you would not be living by the Spirit of Christ. You would be living according to the law and Pharisaism.

Even though some of the Bible is not correct, the witness of Christ is still there. The fact that the Bible has inaccuracies in it does not take away from the beauty of it, but rather enhances it even more.

Many Christians believe that the book of Acts is the guide for a New Testament church. We cannot go back 2,000 years and say that the first church is a model for today's church. I really think it's best for Christians to meet in small groups in their homes. The trouble starts when a group of people decide that they need a building and a paid staff to do the Lord's work, which is usually not the Lord's work, but just a lot of religious busyness that produces nothing but more religious busyness.

Chapter 8
The Apostles' Doctrine and Fundamentalism

People who believe that there are no inaccuracies in the Bible and who live by the Bible are fundamentalists. I have always considered these people to be dangerous. The Spirit of Jesus is totally disregarded and replaced with Scripture. Much of the trouble in the world today is due to religious fundamentalism.

The Pharisees were fundamentalists and lived according to the book. What is amazing, they used the Bible to crucify Christ. They said we have a law, and according to our law, he must die. They got that law out of the Old Testament. It was probably Leviticus 24:16.

Jesus said to the Pharisees, *"Hereafter you shall see the Son of man sitting on the right hand of power, coming in the clouds of heaven."* Matthew 26:64 (KJV Mod.).

That did it; the Pharisees accused Jesus of blasphemy and sentenced him to die. Jesus was condemned by religious Scripture. A true-blue fundamentalist will do anything to uphold Scripture. He may even murder someone to do it. Most fundamentalists believe that the Bible is the word of God; that is, it is God breathed. Because it is God breathed, fundamentalists believe it is inerrant, or without error. If it was God breathed, it would probably be inerrant, but you see, God used sinful men to write the Bible. Men make mistakes. Sometimes men hear things backwards. However, the Scriptures are very accurate about who Jesus Christ is and what he has done on our behalf. This part of the Bible is errant and can be believed upon. We don't need a perfect Bible to be saved, but we do need a perfect Christ.

The Pharisees worried over Old Testament Scripture trying to figure out what they might do to make themselves a little more knowledgeable than the next Pharisee. They took pride in knowing the law and being able to quote scripture. Jesus said, *"You search the scriptures, in them you think you have eternal life."* John 5:39 (KJV Mod.). The unfortunate thing is that they missed the Scripture that testified of Christ. This is the trait of a typical fundamentalist. They are so busy searching Scripture for something to *do* that they miss what's been *done* for them by Christ.

Paul said *"For they are ignorant of God's righteousness and they go about trying to establish their own righteousness."* Romans 10:3 (KJV Mod.). This is why we can't leave the Gospel behind and try to go into holy living. We must always live in the light of the Gospel.

Two men went up to the Temple to pray. One was a Pharisee, the other a Publican. Publicans were thought to be the scum of the earth. The Pharisee stood and prayed, "Thank God, I'm not like other men, extortionists, unjust, adulterers, sinners, or even like this Publican. I fast twice a week; I give tithes of all I possess, I'm really a righteous fellow."

Scripture says that the Publican could not even look up, but smote himself on his chest saying, "Oh God, be merciful to me, a sinner, for I have no righteousness." Luke 18:10-13 (KJV Mod.).

Most Christians do not like to be identified as fundamentalists, because they don't want to be thought of as closed-minded or make dogmatic claims that they possess the truth. Fundamentalists see themselves as people of the book and their religion is a religion of the book.

The blackest word heard in a fundamentalist's vocabulary is the word "compromise." The fundamentalist is a purest, a man of principal, a man who lives according to the book. The first fundamentalists were the Pharisees. The spirit of Jesus was offensive to the Pharisees because of the freedom that it portrayed.

Can you imagine what they thought when Jesus and his disciples were walking through the cornfield on the Sabbath day, shucking corn. The Pharisees thought that their obligation was to do the will of God as expressed in the Old Testament Scripture. When Jesus called them hypocrites, this cut them through the heart. (Matthew 23:15). Because that was one of their worst sins. They obeyed the Scripture no matter what. This is what made them hypocrites.

A good example of this is in the Parable of the Good Samaritan. It was against Scripture for the Pharisees to touch a bloody man, so when they saw him in the ditch, they crossed over to the other side of the road to avoid even looking at him. (Luke 10:30-37). This is a classic case of fundamentalism and why it can make you a hypocrite.

The rest of the story shows us what the spirit of Jesus is like. The Samaritan bound up his wounds, took him to a hotel and told the man at the desk, here is money to take care of him. If it's not enough, I will come by later and take care of it. Which spirit was right? Which spirit was wrong?

It's easy to be a monk and live in a monastery away from the world, just you, the Bible and Jesus. But that's not the kind of Christian the Lord wants us to be. We are supposed to be out there in the world, applying bandages to bloody wounds, pulling people out of the ditches of life. Jesus tells a parable about a king that invited his subjects to come and inherit his kingdom. He said to them, *"I was hungry and you gave me meat. I was thirsty and you gave me drink. I was a stranger and you took me in. I was naked and you clothed me. I was sick and you visited me. I was in prison and you came to see me. And his subjects said, 'Lord, when did we see you in need of these things?' and the king said, 'In as much as you have done it unto the very least of these my brethren, you have done it unto me.'* Matthew 25:34-46 (KJV Mod.).

Serving the Lord means being involved with people. The Pharisees thought of themselves as being too holy to get involved with people, so they lived in their little monasteries away from the needs of others; just them, the Torah, and God.

Most Christians are so busy with church activities that they don't have time to get involved with people outside the church. I used to go to church five times a week. There was always something going on. I should have been down at the homeless mission doing volunteer work.

Fundamentalism is an introverted religion. The reason for this is because you have to maintain your piety. This takes time and effort. Jesus said, *"Woe unto you Scribes and Pharisees; hypocrites, you encompass land and sea to make one like yourself and when he is made, he is twice the child of hell that you are."* Matthew 23:15 (KJV Mod.).

Chapter 9
The Apostles' Doctrine and Antichrist

What is Antichrist? We know for sure that Satan is Antichrist. We might even say that Antichrist is his chief, or main preoccupation. Satan is the mighty deceiver. His work is to subvert the message of Christ. He does this by blinding people to truth. Even though spiritually speaking he is a defeated foe, he is still alive and well and doing a great job, as we shall see.

You would think that because the Son of God came to this earth and died on a wooden cross, that everyone would want to know why, or what does this mean to me? The whole world is indifferent to this subject. It's like the human race is on a sinking ship and no one cares. It reminds me of the movie of the Titanic. Everyone was partying and enjoying themselves, even after they knew the ship was sinking. What has lulled the world into this state of complacency? It's almost as if people are in some sort of a hypnotic trance on their way to hell.

The Apostle John had a lot to say about Antichrist. He said, *"These are the last days, as you have heard, that the Antichrist shall come, and even now there are many Antichrist's. By this we know that these are the last days."* 1st John 2:18, (KJV Mod.). Everything after the Christ event are the last days. John associates the last days with many Antichrist's.

Paul wrote, *"Let no man deceive you by any means, for that day shall not come except their come a falling away first."* 2nd Thessalonians 1:3 (KJV Mod.). It appears that as we get closer to the coming of Christ, many will be deceived by Antichrist's.

How can we identify Antichrist's so that we will not be deceived? John wrote, *"Don't believe every spirit, but try the spirits to see if it's of God."* And how do we try the spirit? We test them in the light of the Gospel.

Jesus came into this world as the God-man. Our humanity was in him. As a new Adam and representative of the human race, he offered to God a life of perfect obedience to God's will. It's the only life that God will accept. God accepts the life of Christ on our behalf, just as though we had lived it ourselves. In his death, again our humanity was in him. When he died, we died with him. This was a fulfillment of the law. The soul that sins must die. (See Ezekiel 18:20 (KJV Mod.).

Christ took our death upon himself and died in our place and on our behalf. When Christ arose from the dead, we arose with him. (See Romans 5:17, 6:3, 6:5, 6:8). God accepted the life, death and resurrection of Christ on our behalf. Just as though we had lived, died and rose again, our salvation is safe and secure because it is at the right hand of God in heaven. This is the Apostle's doctrine of the Gospel of Jesus Christ. Everything should be tried in the light of this Gospel; every doctrine must be tested by this Gospel. All must come into question by this Gospel. Satan does not want us to know or understand this message. He wants us to be religious and try to go to heaven by our own works and piety, which we can't do.

There is only one way to be saved, and that is by being in Christ, accept his life, death and resurrection. Make it yours. It's the greatest gift that God can give you. Repent of your own effort to be righteous. Confess that you are a sinner and need his salvation. *"For by Grace, (God's goodness), are you saved, through faith and not that of yourselves. It is a gift of God."* Ephesians 2:8 (KJV Mod.).

The purpose of the Bible is to reveal Jesus Christ. Scripture is also full of warnings about false teachers, Antichrist's and those who would pervert the Gospel. We should pay careful attention to these verses. The world is full of deceivers. Revelation says, *"The great dragon was cast out, that old serpent called the devil, and Satan, which deceives the whole world, was cast out into the earth and his angels were cast out with him."* Revelation 12:9 (KJV Mod.).

Millions of people think that they are without sin and that they are going to go to heaven on their own merit. This is exactly what Satan wants us to believe. The world says, "you're okay, I'm okay. Everything is okay." The Scripture says just the opposite. *"All have sinned and come short of the glory of God."* Romans 3:23 (KJV Mod.).

As it is written, *"There is none righteous, no not one."* Romans 3:10 (KJV Mod.). I would like to differ with this last scripture, because there was one righteous, his name was Jesus Christ. He was not born after Adam, he was born after God. He is the only one that you can trust and put your faith in.

Paul also said, *"By the deeds of the law* (or by being religious) *no flesh will be justified in his sight."* Romans 3:20 (KJV Mod.). Antichrist wants you to believe that because you are a good person, you are going to be okay. Wrong. Without Christ, you are in danger of hell-fire.

Satan is very clever. He doesn't deny that Christ came into the world. That would be such an obvious lie. No, instead he will take a good thing and put it in place of the very best thing. This is a very deceitful move. You think you have the best, but you don't. You just have something good that you think is the very best. As long as you think you have the best when you don't, Satan is very happy and he has accomplished his purpose.

Religion can be a good thing, many will say. Look at all the good things that religion does. We have many religious hospitals, rest homes, homeless missions. Surely all this is not bad, but it is a good thing! I agree it is a good thing, but it is not the best.

I've always questioned religious works. What is the motivational factor for a certain denomination to build a hospital or retirement home? It's usually money, not gratitude for what Christ has done, even though it's a good work and everyone will say, "look, we do good things." Yes, they do it for money. The Gospel is the very best thing. Nothing compares to what Christ has accomplished for us.

It is the pearl of great price that a man sells all that he owns to purchase. It is the greatest gift that God has given to the human race. Every prayer that has been prayed, God answered when he gave us Christ. My question is, why do you want second best when you can have the very best? Of course, there is not much glory in being a Gospel-believing Christian, because Christ did it all. We just simply rest in his work.

Whereas if you are religious, you can talk about all kinds of things. I even heard a testimony one time about this fellow that ran out of gas in his truck. After a few moments of feverish prayer, God put in a quarter of a tank so he could get to a gas station. I guess religion is fun because you can always come up with some sort of mystical nonsense to impress your friends. Religious people like to play, "can you top this miracle?" I always wondered why God didn't give him a full tank. Maybe that would have been too hard to believe.

I've sat in church and heard some of the most stupid, ridiculous statements come out of Christians mouths that you could dream of. This kind of thing doesn't bring glory to Christ. As a matter o fact, I consider it to be Antichrist. There are no miracles, at least not from the Lord. There are no revelations. If you believe in miracles and revelations, then you must believe that the Bible is not a finished work and the Lord has something further to communicate to us. He has said all that he is going to say.

The Scripture says that in these last days God has spoken to us by his Son. When God gave us Christ, he said all that he is going to say. (See Hebrews 1:1-2). There is no further word. A miracle means that the Lord is communicating something new to us. A new revelation, which there is none. Jesus said, *"An evil and adulterous generation seeks after a sign. But no sign shall be given."* Matthew 12:39 (KJV Mod.).

God does not want to detract from what Christ has accomplished for us. If there were more signs and miracles and revelations, it would be about Christ and his Gospel. The call is to live by faith, that is, faith in Christ. If you need signs, miracles, revelations, maybe you don't have faith. I don't have to stick my finger in an electrical socket to believe that I will be shocked. I know by faith that the electrical current is there. If you have to have miracles to believe, sorry, but you don't have faith.

Jesus said, *"Beware of men."* Matthew 10:17 (KJV Mod.). There are many well-meaning pastors that have been to the seminary, but they didn't get the truth there. Most seminaries teach systematic theology. Just the name systematic is a tip off that something might be wrong. There is no system in the Gospel. The Gospel is about what Christ has accomplished on behalf of sinners.

In systematic theology, the focus is on the cross. Systematic theology starts with a cross and builds from there. The Apostles' doctrine starts with the resurrection. The cross of Christ was a good thing for us, but the resurrection was the best. Please take note that most churches have a cross on their steeple. The Catholic Church takes it a step further by placing Christ on the cross. I think that it would be correct to say that the evangelical church is obsessed with the death of Christ. To take it even a step further, organized religion is a religion of death. In the Catholic religion, it is death and blood. Perhaps this is why the priest wears black.

As we pointed out earlier, Antichrist places something good in the place of what is the best. The resurrection is what turned the world upside down. The Apostles were not running all over Jerusalem talking about the death of Christ. No, they were telling everyone about the resurrection. As Peter said, *"We ought to obey God rather than men. The God of our fathers has raised up Jesus whom you have killed and hanged on a tree and God has exalted him, placing him at his right hand to be Prince and Saviour. So as to give repentance and forgiveness of sins to Israel. We are witnesses of these things and so is the Holy Ghost whom God has given to them that obey him."* The Scripture goes on to say that when the Pharisees heard this, they were cut to the heart and took council on how they could kill them, (see Acts 5:29-33).

There is no victory in a dead Christ. I resent seeing Christ on a cross. There is nothing sacred about it. Nor do I like to see a manger scene. Christ is not in a manger, nor is he on a cross. Why portray him in such a way? What if every time you had a birthday they drug out all your baby pictures and showed them around and talked about your babyhood. I don't think you would like it. Christ exalted to the right hand of God brings glory to him. This gives him his rightful place.

There is an attempt today to dethrone the Son of God by bringing him down and placing him in the human heart. How many times have you heard someone say, "What is Jesus doing in you life?" (Like he is living another life in and through the believer). The Bible knows nothing of this kind of doctrine, nor does it bring glory to Jesus. If anything, it degrades him by bringing him down into the human existence. Why would Jesus, who is pure and without sin, want to live in and through a sinner?

The work of the Spirit is a separate work, apart from the work of the Son. The work of Jesus is that of Saviour. The work of the Spirit is to glorify that work and to draw us to Christ. It is bad doctrine to confuse the two. The Bible doesn't do it, the Apostles didn't do it, nor should we do it.

The Catholic Church has had an influence on the Protestant churches in this area. They teach that the more you take the sacraments, which represent the flesh and blood of Jesus, the more you will become like him. This is a damnable heresy. No matter what you do, you can never be like Christ.

Isaiah said, *"We are all as an unclean thing and all of our righteousness are like filthy rags."* Isaiah 64:6. (KJV Mod.). Paul wrote *"All have sinned and come short of the glory of God."* Romans 3:23 (KJV Mod.).

But many will say, "Yes, I was a sinner but I repented and became a Christian and now I am okay." If this is what you think, you are the worst kind of a sinner. You are now a religious sinner. It was religious sinners that had Christ crucified. You need to repent from that kind of thinking and accept the fact that you are still a sinner, desperately in need of God's grace and Christ's salvation.

As Christians, we live our lives before the Lord as sinners. Many would have you believe that you can attain unto some kind of righteousness that God will accept. If that was the case, the saving work of Christ was in vain. Sanctification never comes ahead of justification. We always live in the light of the Gospel. We are always sinners.

Antichrist would have you believe that there is another way to be saved. There is only one Gospel, there is only one Spirit. Jesus is the only way. The Holy Spirit will not save you. That is not his work.

Antichrist likes to mix up the Trinity so that you will become confused. Each entity of the Trinity has a separate function or a separate work. Antichrist will place more importance upon the work of the Holy Spirit in the believer than the work of Christ outside of the believer. Something good in the place of what is best. How many books have been written about the work of the Holy Spirit? It must be in the thousands. How many on the work of Christ? I doubt if you can find one, except this one.

The work of the Spirit is subjective. The work of Christ is objective. The work of the Spirit is ongoing. He convinces us of sin and points us to Christ. The work of Christ is a finished work. Before Jesus died on the cross, he said, *"It is finished."* John 19:30 (KJV Mod.). All that was necessary to save the human race has been completed.

Paul wrote and said, *"You are complete in him."* Colossians 2:10 (KJV Mod.). You cannot make yourself any better than what Christ has made you. It is not the work of the Spirit to make you righteous. You may live a better life because of the Spirit because we now understand what it cost Christ to save us from sin. This should cause us to turn from sin or to repent. Antichrist would have you more concerned about what the Spirit is doing in your life than what Christ has done outside of your life.

There are a great number of Christians who think that the Lord talks to them inside of their head. This thinking can get you into a whole lot of trouble. How many times have you heard some murderer tell the police that "a voice inside their head told them to kill someone." My question is when you hear a voice inside your head, how do you know who it is? Is it the Lord, or is it the devil? Or maybe it's your own thinking? How do you know the difference. It's best not to listen to voices.

This hearing of voices is called mysticism. Do not rely upon feelings. The Lord gave us a brain to figure things out. Voices and feelings can lead you astray. I've heard numerous testimonies in churches on how the Lord led someone to do something. They never say exactly how this happened. Did they hear a voice, or was it a feeling?

Pastors are famous for having a testimony on how the Lord called them into the ministry. What I find to be strange is that many of these pastors don't know what the Gospel is. Just because we have a strong feeling to do something doesn't necessarily mean that we have been called. Sometimes money or prestige is the motivating factor. As far as preaching the Gospel, we are all called to do that providing you know what the Gospel is. This is part of the work of the Holy Spirit in the life of the believer.

If you really believe the Gospel, you are going to have to talk about it to someone. The message is so great and it is such good news that it is impossible to keep it to yourself. You may even be like John and Peter when they said, *"We cannot but speak of the things which we have seen and heard."* Acts 4:20 (KJV Mod.).

Ever since I've learned the Gospel, I've not been the same. I must say with the Apostle Paul that *"Though I preach the Gospel, I have nothing to glory of for necessity is laid upon me. Yes, woe is unto me if I do not preach the Gospel."* 1st Corinthians 9:16. (KJV Mod.).

I guess this is my testimony. I've come to the conclusion that organized religion is Antichrist or anti-Gospel. Organized religion cannot co-exist with the Gospel. Nor is the Gospel compatible with a hierarchy. The Gospel makes us all even in Christ, or all equal. We all have the same revelation of him. There is none greater and none lesser. Religion can not exist without a hierarchy. Someone must mediate the religious articles or the creeds.

All religions have their popes and it is the business of these popes to sustain the religion. Gospel believing Christians do not need popes or religions. The Scripture *says "There is one mediator between Man and God and that is Jesus Christ."* 1st Timothy 2:5 (KJV Mod.). We enter a very dangerous area when we rely upon a man to tell us what we should believe.

The Bible was written for the common man. If one has trouble knowing what they believe, they should turn to the Scriptures. The writings of the Apostle Paul makes it very clear what the Gospel is. The book of Romans, especially the 5th and 6th chapters makes it very clear that Christ is the new Adam and we are crucified, buried and risen in him.

Paul wrote that *"We should not be like children tossed to and fro and carried about with every wind of doctrine by the slight of men and cunning craftiness where they lie in wait to deceive you."* Ephesians 4:14. (KJV Mod.). We should know what we believe and believe what we know to be the truth. Paul said, *"I know in whom I have believed and that he is able to keep that which I've committed onto him."* 2nd Timothy 1:12 (KJV Mod.).

False teachers take advantage of Christians because Christians have a struggle with sin in their lives. This is a normal part of being a Christian. There is no solution to this problem. The only strength comes from knowing that God has already dealt with the sin problem in the person of Jesus Christ. Paul said, *"O wretched man that I am. Who shall deliver me from this body of death? I thank God it has been done through Jesus Christ our Lord. So then with my mind I serve the law of God but with my flesh, the law of sin."* Romans 7:24-25 (KJV Mod.). Paul also said he was the "chief of all sinners" (see 1st Timothy 1:15).

The holiness movement is Antichrist. They don't need the Gospel. Only sinners need the Gospel. Jesus said that he came into the world to save sinners. The question is, do you qualify? We are all sinners without works because we are all born sinners. I know this is hard to accept, especially when it is a cute little baby that has been born, but sooner or later that cute little baby will grow up and then you will know for sure that this is a sinner. It's okay to be a sinner. Accept your sinner-hood. We are all sinners without works. That is, we don't have to prove we are sinners; it just comes naturally.

As we are sinners without works, we are also saved without works. So relax, enjoy your sinnerhood, but please keep in mind that there can be dire consequences in acting out your sinful desires.

Chapter 10
The Apostles' Doctrine and Faith

There are approximately four hundred and eighty references to faith in the Bible, most of which are in the New Testament. What is faith? Faith is the glue of Christianity. Faith is our part. This is something that we do. The Gospel is about what Christ has done outside of us. Faith is a subjective thing that happens within the believer. We can have a lot of faith, or we can have little faith, or we can have no faith.

Faith usually precedes belief. We hear the Gospel and we say, "That's nice." But when we take hold of it and make it ours, that's faith. As an example: for years, I knew about Christ, I had a belief in him, but that is as far as it went. When I was convicted by the Spirit that I needed Jesus, faith took hold and I reached out to him. This was an act of faith.

Another example was on the day of Pentecost. All of the Apostles were in one place. Did they know what Christ had done for them in his life, death and resurrection? No, but they did have a belief in him. They knew that he was the Son of God. They thought he was going to come back, overthrow the Romans and establish His Kingdom. (See Acts 1:6).

They remembered what the two men in white had said to them when Jesus ascended, *"You men of Galilee. Why are you standing here looking up into heaven? This same Jesus which was taken up shall also return in like manner."* Acts 1:10-11 (KJV Mod.).

The Apostles were preparing to rule and reign with Christ. What came on the day of Pentecost was a complete surprise to them. The sound came from heaven like a rushing, mighty wind, and the cloven tongues of fire and men were speaking a different language other than their own. It must have been absolute chaos!

Acts 2:12 (KJV Mod.) says, they were all amazed and were in doubt, saying one to another, 'What does all of this mean?" It was not until Peter stood up and preached the Gospel that they knew what it was all about. When the people heard about the wonderful works of God, they were pricked in their hearts. The Holy Spirit had revealed all that Christ had done to save them from their sins. And they said, "What are we going to do?" (see Acts 2:37). Then Peter said, "Repent and be baptized in the name of Jesus for the remission of sins." Faith in Jesus had been kindled in their hearts. They reached out to him in faith. Faith in Christ calls for a response. The response was, "What must we do?" Acts 4:4 says *"That as many that heard the word, that is, the Gospel, believed; and the number was about five thousand."*

Paul wrote, *"For whosoever shall call upon the name of the Lord shall be saved. How then shall they call on him in whom they have not believed? How should they believe in him on whom they have not heard?"* Acts 10:14 (KJV Mod.). *"So then, faith comes then by hearing, and hearing by the Word of God."* which is the Gospel. Acts 10:17 (KJV Mod.).

I am convinced that there are a lot of people that have heard about Christ and the Gospel, but they are not Christians. The Scripture says *"For the heart of these people is waxed gross and their ears are dull of hearing and their eyes are closed, lest they should hear with their ears, see with their eyes and understand with their heart and be converted."* Acts 28:27 (KJV Mod.).

I guess what I am saying is that you must be affected by this Gospel. It is not enough to hear it, it must be meaningful to you to the point that you are motivated by it. As the fiery Apostle James said, *"What does it profit a man if he says he has faith and does not have works? Can faith save him? Even so, faith if it doesn't have works is dead."* James 2:14-17 (KJV Mod.).

Now some will say, "What kind of works shall I do to show that I have faith? Does this mean that I have to become a missionary to become a Christian?"

There is a story about a man that had two dogs. The dogs were talking one day about the man. One said, "You know, I think our master has become a Christian."

The other dog said, "What makes you say that?"

"Well, you know how we used to lay out on the front porch and every time he walked by he would give us a swift kick."

"Yeah." Said the other dog.

"Well, he stopped doing that. Now have you noticed that he leans down and pats us on the head when he passes by?"

Sometimes doing good works does not necessarily mean doing a great thing. It may mean doing a good thing, like being a responsible person, or trying to be a better father or mother, perhaps being more considerate of others. When you are kind to others, it is like being kind to Christ.

When Paul was converted on the way to Damascus, Jesus said to Paul, *"Why are you persecuting me, Paul? It is hard for you to kick against the pricks."* Acts 9:5 (KJV Mod.). Have you ever tried kicking something sharp or uneven? It us usually not a good idea to kick anything, much less to kick something that is going to hurt you or injure you. Jesus was really saying, "Paul, why are you going against me? You will only injure yourself." We should follow the leading of the Spirit of Jesus in our lives.

Someone might say, "What is the leading of the Spirit of Jesus?" That's easily answered: does it show love and compassion? Is it a thing that is good for all? Does it show mercy? Is it a help to someone? Is it truthful? Does it honor Christ? This is the Spirit of Jesus.

If you go against the Spirit, you are the one that will suffer. As Jesus said, "It is hard to kick against the pricks." Where there is faith in Christ, there is the Spirit, also. They are like companions. Paul said to the Galatians, *"This only what I learn of you. Did you receive the Spirit by the works of the law or by hearing the Gospel?"* Galatians 3:2 (KJV Mod.). We hear the Gospel and the Spirit comes to confirm our faith in what we have heard.

Sometimes I think that the Lord is testing me to see if I really have faith. I'm sure that many of you feel the same way. We all have things happen in our lives that make us wonder if we are really one of his children.

I had a serious abdominal surgery a few years ago and as I laid in that hospital bed completely absorbed in pain and discomfort, I thought about Christ on the cross hanging there for me in much more pain than I was suffering. But the pain was not the worst thing. The worst thing was that I felt forsaken. So it is with us when trials and tribulations come our way. We cry out also, "My God, why have you forsaken me?" Peter wrote, *"Beloved, don't think that some strange thing is happened to you when you are going through a fiery trial. This has happened to test you. But rejoice because you are partakers of Christ's suffering."* Galatians 4:12-13 (KJV Mod.).

God tested Job's faith. Satan spoke through Job's wife when she said to Job, *"Why don't you curse God and die?"* Job 2:9 (KJV Mod.). But Job kept his faith and said, *"Even though he slays me, yet will I trust in him."* Job 13:15 (KJV Mod.).

Paul wrote, *"What shall separate us from the love of Christ? Shall tribulation or distress or persecution or famine or nakedness or peril or sword? As it is written for your sake we are killed all the day long. We are counted as sheep for the slaughter. No, in all these things we are more than conquerors through him that loves us. For I am persuaded that neither life nor death nor angels nor principalities nor powers nor things present, nor things to come, nor height or depth, or any creature shall be able to separate us from the love of God, which is in Christ Jesus, our Lord."* Romans 8:35-39 (KJV Mod.).

The mark of Christ is his Spirit. All who are his, have his mark. The Spirit brings faith in Christ and his work for us. We never leave that behind, but rather we live in it.

Abraham was also tested by the Lord. The Lord said to Abraham, "Take now your son, your only son whom you love, Isaac, and take him to the land of Moriah and offer him there upon a mountain which I will show you." Abraham rose up early, packed up some wood, took two men and Isaac with him and went to the place where the Lord had told him. And Abraham told the two men to stay behind and he took Isaac and the wood and fire and a knife and went up on the mountain.

When they got there, Isaac said, "I see that we have the fire and the wood, but where is the lamb for the burnt offering?" Abraham laid out the wood, tied up Isaac and laid him upon the altar of wood.   Abraham took his knife, raised his hand to slay Isaac. When an angel of the Lord said, "Stop! Don't do it! I know now that you fear God and have faith in him."   What a test!   Did Abraham believe God would bring Isaac back to life?   We don't know.

There are other great men of faith in the Bible.   Another is Noah, who was warned by the Lord of things to come. He built an ark on dry land to save his family. Moses chose to suffer affliction with the people of God rather than be called the son of Pharaoh's daughter. Moses forsook Egypt, not fearing the wrath of the king.

There are many other good examples. A good book to read is Hebrews, the 11th chapter. They were saved in the Old Testament the same way that we are saved today, by faith alone.

The only difference is that they looked forward, whereas we look back.

The Scripture says *"They were stoned, they were sawn in two, they were tempted, they were slain with a sword. They wandered about in sheepskins and goatskins, being destitute, afflicted, torment-ed, of whom the world was not worthy. They wandered in the deserts and in the mountains, and in the dens and caves of the earth. And all of these having obtained a good report of faith, did not receive the promise."* Hebrews 11:37-39 (KJV Mod.).

The promise was that of a Saviour. They looked forward to the day when God would provide a Saviour. We are much more fortu-nate than they are, because we know who the Saviour is and what he has accomplished on our behalf. We also have a New Testament that tells about him.

The most fortunate, are the Apostles. John wrote, *"That which was from the beginning, we have heard him, and with our eyes we have een him. With our hands we have touched him, for we have seen this* *fe and bear witness to it and declare it unto you that this is the eter-* *al life which was manifested unto us that was with the Father."* st John 1:1-2 (KJV Mod.).

So there are three kinds of faith: hands on faith, forward faith, nd backward faith. We are the blessed ones. Jesus said to ¯homas, *"Blessed are they which have not seen me, yet believe in me."* ohn 20:29 (KJV Mod.).

As the Scripture says, *"Faith is the substance of things hoped for,* *¹e evidence of things not seen."* Hebrews 11:1 (KJV Mod.). The .ord wants us to live by faith, believing and trusting in him; rely- ng upon him, depending upon him, seeking after him. This is 1ow we are to live: not by mysticism, revelations, signs or miracles. ¯hese things are not of faith and are most certainly not of the ·pirit.

Again I say, the Christian faith is objective. It goes outside of 1s to Christ. Mysticism, revelations, signs and miracles are subjec- ive things. I refer to them as things of the flesh, or of religion. ¯hese are the things that cause divisions within a church or a body ·f believers. Pride is never more prominent than when someone 1inks that they have gotten a private word from the Lord, or a pri- ate revelation. Especially when all of us poor unspiritual sinners lon't hear anything or don't see anything.

I used to think that there was something wrong with my ¯hristian life because nothing was happening. No voices, no signs, 10 revelations, and no miracles. I thought, "Oh well, I must be a econd-class Christian. I guess I will have to get the sin out of my fe so I can become a super-duper Christian." Believe me when I ay, there are multitudes of teachers just waiting to help you do 1is.

I always look at these teachers as Pharisees. Jesus said to the Pharisees, *"You go over land and see to make one prostilite and when he is made, he is twice the child of hell that you are."* Matthew 23:15 (KJV Mod.).

I know that I've probably lost some of you after the last few paragraphs. This is unfortunate, because you are the ones that need to read this book. Faith is a God-given gift. It is not something that we muster up.

Even if you are not a Christian, faith is still present in your life. You may have faith in your friends, or faith in a spouse, or maybe even faith in the government. I have never met anyone who didn't have faith in something. Sometimes when I hear about some of the things that people have faith in, I am amazed! Especially some of the religions with huge memberships that are cults. It would be easier for me to have faith in Snow White and the Seven Dwarfs than to have faith in these weird religions. Education, or having high intelligence, doesn't seem to matter. Maybe that's part of the problem.

Paul charges Timothy to *"Fight the good fight of faith, lay hold unto eternal life unto which you have been called and have a good profession of faith before many witnesses."* 1st Timothy 6:12 (KJV Mod.). In other words, Timothy, live like what you believe. The Gospel calls for that. There are many people watching you to see if you can really live what you believe. Nothing hurts the Gospel more than someone who professes faith in Christ and then goes out and lives like the devil.

I had a friend who was a professing Christian. His name was Jack. Every time something went wrong, it was, "God damn this or God damn that." I called him over to the side one day and said, "Jack, I know that you profess faith in Christ and you say that you are a Christian. I don't know why, and maybe you can tell me why, you are always damning something in the name of the Lord."

He said, "I'm sorry, Bob, I can't help it."

I said, "Jack, maybe you shouldn't tell people that you are a Christian until you get this 'damning' thing under control." He agreed with me and he eventually stopped cursing in the name of the Lord, but it took him a while.

The reason we live the Christian life is not to be holy so that the Lord will accept us or bless us, we live Christian lives so that others will see that we have faith in Christ and his Gospel.

This is why Paul is always exhorting Christians to live above sin. A good example of this is found in Acts, Chapter 5. The Gospel had just come into the world. The Apostles had been called of God to preach the Gospel. Many people were selling their possessions so that the Apostles could go forth and preach the Gospel. (see Acts 4:34-37).

There was a couple named Ananias and Sapphria. The Scripture says that they sold a possession to give to the Apostles, but secretly held back part of the money for themselves. As a result of this act, both of them died instantly. The Scripture says that great fear came upon all the church that heard this. (See Acts 5:1-11).

It is a serious thing when someone professes faith in Christ and then does something to damage the Gospel. I guess what I'm saying is, if you can't live it, don't preach it. There is one thing the Lord really hates and that is a hypocrite.

Have you ever noticed that those people that are a part of the holiness movement have trouble in their lives? A good example is

Jim Baker. There was no gospel in his ministry, and I mean the whole Gospel, not just that our sins were on Christ and God punished Christ in our place. I mean the life, death and resurrection for us and on our behalf. I mean, being made righteous by Christ by his work and not our own. Jim Baker had no strength in his life because he had no Gospel.

We who are Gospel believing Christians, want to uphold this Gospel. It's meaningful to us. We don't want to disgrace Christ and his work for us. We want to honor it with our lives. This is called, living the Christian life. The purpose of teaching in the church should be to build faith in Christ and his Gospel.

In all of Paul's epistles, he is always trying to bring the churches back to the Gospel. He would visit the churches, ground them in the Gospel and then go off to visit another church to teach the Gospel to them also. And then the word would come to Paul about the church that had been grounded in the Gospel, how they had allowed the Judaizers in to confuse the Gospel with Law.

So Paul would write a letter. A good example is a letter to the Galatians where he wrote, *"I marvel that you are so soon removed from him that called you into the Grace of Christ into another Gospel which is not another, but there be some that trouble you and would pervert the Gospel of Christ."* Galatians 1:6-7 (KJV Mod.).

Paul was very busy trying to keep the churches grounded in the Gospel. We all have a tendency to become religious and forget the Gospel. I think this is part of our sin nature that we should leave the Gospel behind and go off into Christian living. This thinking is very prevalent in organized religion. The Gospel, if they have one, is always secondary to Christian living and soon they have lost sight of it completely.

Paul wrote, *"We should continue in the Gospel and not be moved away from it."* Colossians 1:23 (KJV Mod.). Again, Satan draws our focus away to something good, but it is not the best. The Gospel is the very best. It is from this that our Christian lives have their root and strength. Even though our faith is important, it's not the most important thing in our lives. We should not focus to much on how much or how little faith that we have. Our focus should always be on Christ and his faithfulness to us. Paul wrote, *'Let us hold fast the profession of our faith without wavering, for he is faithful, that promised."* Hebrews 10:23 (KJV Mod.).

Jesus was faithful to God in his work as the Saviour of humanty. Everything he did was to please God and he did it for us and on our behalf. He was the faithful Saviour that took away the sins of the world.

The Apostles said, "Lord, increase our faith." And Jesus said, *'If you had faith the size of a mustard seed, you might say to this sycamore tree 'be plucked up by the root and be planted by the sea' and it would obey you."* Luke 17:5-6 (KJV Mod.). So the Apostles didn't have much faith. Neither do we.

I don't believe in faith healers. However, there are some people who have been healed because they believed they were going to overcome their sickness and be well again. Some of these people are not even Christians. They simply have faith that they were going to get well. Faith and positive thinking can do wonders in a person's life.

We should always have faith and think positive no matter what comes into our lives. Sometimes bad things have a way of turning out for the best. As Paul said, *"We know that all things work together for good to them that love God, to them who are called according to his purpose."* Romans 8:28 (KJV Mod.).

This doesn't mean that when we screw something up that the Lord will unscrew it for us. There are consequences to wrong or foolish decisions and choices. Sometimes we will have to reap the whirlwind. But in the long run, all things work together for our good.

Chapter 11
The Apostles' Doctrine and the Law

The words law and religion are interchangeable. That is, in most cases, they mean the same thing. When we are doing the law, we are practicing religion. When we are religious, we are doing the law. The law says do. It is a command to do something or to perform a religious act. Sometimes the Lord used the law to make a covenant with Israel. Sometimes when the Lord gave the law, it was not to do something. In the case of Adam, the Lord said, *"Of every tree of the garden, you may eat freely. But of the tree of knowledge of good and evil, do not eat of it. For the day that you eat of it, you shall surely die."* (The death was eternal separation from God.) Genesis 2:16-17 (KJV Mod.).

I think that the first thing that Adam did after he had heard this commandment was to go take a look at the tree. There is something in human nature, that the minute we are told not to do something, we want to do it. I suppose this is part of our sin nature. It wasn't long until Adam was eating the fruit from the tree of knowledge of good and evil.

Was this the beginning of religion? God had made a covenant with Adam. The garden and everything in it was for Adam. All Adam had to do was obey the law, which God had given to him. There was more or less an agreement between God and Adam. Did Adam think that when he ate of the tree that he would be like God?

Why do people study religion? Would I be right in saying that people study religion to be holy like God? Regardless of what

Adam's motive was in eating the forbidden fruit, he apparently wanted to break the covenant that he had with God. However, I don't think he really understood the total consequences of his actions.

Adam was driven out of the garden by the Lord never to return again. Naturally, he blamed everything on Eve. We always look for an excuse when we sin or blame it on someone else. I'm sure that he also said, "The devil made me do it."

Adam was the first father of the human race. Everyone born after Adam is a sinner, just like Adam. We are all covenant breakers. Because of Adam's failure, we all live in a fallen universe and we are all members of a fallen race.

Scripture says, *"Wherefore as by one man, sin entered into the world and death by sin, so death passed upon all men for that all have sinned."* Romans 5:12 (KJV Mod.). *"For as by one man's disobedience, many were made sinners (Adam) so by the obedience of one (Christ) shall many be made righteous."* Romans 5:19 (KJV Mod.).

Christ came into the world and undid what Adam had done. Christ was the new Adam. He offered perfect obedience to God's law and in our name and on our behalf. Read Romans Chapters 5 and 6. I consider these two chapters to be the most important chapters in the Bible. You may think God was unfair in his dealings with Adam. The way I look at it: this is God's world. We are God's creatures. If this is how he wants us to play the game, I guess we had better play by his rules. Like he told Paul, "It's hard to kick against the pricks." It's best to follow the rules or laws he has set before us. *"The way of the transgressor is hard."* Proverbs 13:15 (KJV Mod.).

There are over one million men in prison in the United States violators of the law and there are probably another million or two who should be in prison. There are several purposes of the law: for one, it reveals the righteousness of Christ. It also reveals the unrighteousness of man. Paul wrote, *"The law was our schoolmaster to bring us to Christ."* Galatians 3:24 (KJV Mod.). Unfortunately, not all who hear the law come to Christ. I've watched people grit their teeth and clench their fist when they are confronted with the law and their inability to do it, because once you understand that you have fallen short of what God requires, you may need a Saviour. If we never admit this, we can never be saved.

This was the problem the Pharisees had. They thought they were keeping the law and that they were okay. This is the very worst kind of sinner, a religious sinner, one who refuses to admit that he has fallen short of what the law requires.

What does the law require? The two main pillars of the law are: you must love God with all your heart, mind and strength and love your neighbor as yourself. If you fail at this, just one time, you are sinner, worthy of death. Christ offered this to God in our name and on our behalf. The Pharisees took the Ten Commandments and came up with 630 laws or rules to do and to live by. They took a lot of pride in their rule keeping. But that was all it was, rule keeping. They fell short of what the law requires.

One of the most serious violations of the law was that the Pharisees hated the Samaritans who were their neighbors. They also hated anyone that didn't look up to them. Jesus said, *"All the works that they do is so that they can be seen of men."* Matthew 23:5 (KJV Mod.).

They like to stand on street corners and make long prayers so that they can be seen by men. (See Matthew 6:5). Religion can be a showy thing, and pride is never higher than when one is demonstrating his religion or his piety. Have you ever noticed how some religions are so showy that it is almost downright gaudy. I have been in some churches that the inside looks like Disneyland. Churches spend hundreds of thousands of dollars to gaudy up their buildings to try to make them look like some sort of a great, Greek temple. Jesus said, *"When you give, do it secretly."* Matthew 6:4   (KJV Mod.).   And *"when you pray, go into your closet."* Matthew 6:6 (KJV Mod.).

Faith in Christ is not demonstrated in a showy way. That is religion. We who know Christ demonstrate our faith in Christ by what we do, by being compassionate, by love, by helping others. Not in building showy buildings or trying to impress others as to how pious we are. All we really are, are sinners saved by Grace. This should make us humble, not proud like a Pharisee. Paul wrote, *"God has chosen the foolish things of the world to confound the wise and the weak things of the world to confound the mighty."* 1st Corinthians 1:27-28 (KJV Mod.).

The next time you become proud of what you have done, keep in mind it was probably a weak and foolish thing that you did. In a sense, the law is present in the Gospel. When one hears the Gospel and puts their faith in it, it indirectly calls for a response. Like the men on the day of Pentecost when Peter had preached the Gospel to them, their response was, "What shall we do?" Who told them to do anything? No one, but there is a call there to do something.

Some would have you believe that there are two laws: the law of the Old Testament and the law of Christ. They would try to convince us that we are not under the Old Testament law, but we are still under the law of Christ.

I have good news for you, we are not under any law, whether it be Old Testament or the law of Christ. Keep in mind, to be under any law is to be in bondage to religion, and no one can be saved by religion. To be under the law, is a denial of the Gospel. One of the works of Christ was to fulfill the law –that is, to take us out from under the law. Paul said, *"For Christ is the end of the law for righteousness to everyone that believes."* Romans 10:4 (KJV Mod.).

Christ acted on our behalf when he fulfilled the law. We are now under Grace. Does this mean that the law no longer exists? No. It means that we who are Christians will not be judged by it on the Day of Judgment. To be outside of Christ is to be under the law and to be judged by the law and to be condemned by the law.

Paul wrote, *"No man is justified by the law in the sight of God. Whereas it is evident that the just shall live by faith and the law is not of faith but of works."* Galatians 3:11-12 (KJV Mod.).

Does this mean that we can now live as we please, as though there was no law? Yes, but I doubt if you will do that if you are a Christian. Faith brings the Spirit and the Spirit convicts us of sin. I would say that if you want to be one miserable Christian, go out and live like the devil. The misery will be worse than the fun that you think you are having. Paul said the law is not of faith, but the man that does them will live in them."

In other words, now that we don't have to do the law, now that we are free from the law, we will want to obey the law. It's strange, but somehow when we don't have to do something, it's then that we want to do it. Christ is the law personified. We don't want to disappoint our Saviour. We know he is righteous and holy. Paul said, *"For sin shall not have dominion over you, for you are not under the law, but are of Grace. What then, shall we sin because we are not under law but under Grace? God forbid."* Romans 6:14-15 (KJV Mod.).

When we are free from the law, we are also free from sin. For where there is no law, there can be no sin. This may be called, "Living in the Spirit" because we are talking about spiritual things. As Paul said, "There is no condemnation to those who are in Christ." Why?

Because Christ has fulfilled the law, or satisfied the law. That is, to say the demands of the law. *"That the spirit of life in Jesus Christ has made us free from the law of sin and death."* Romans 8: 1-2 (KJV Mod.).

Theoretically speaking, it is not possible for a Christian to sin. Some are now thinking: "Wow, Bob, you have really stuck your foot in it now!" In God's eyes, we have no sin. Not now, not later not forever. Not because of anything that we do, but because of what Christ has accomplished on our behalf. When we stand before the Lord in the Judgment and our name is called to go before the Lord, Christ will walk up and stand in our place. That is, if we are a Christian. If you are not, you will have to stand before the Lord in all of your sins and be condemned to hell.

As Paul said, *"How shall we escape if we neglect so great a salvation?"* Hebrews 2:3 ((KJV Mod.). We won't escape. *"We shall all stand in the judgment."* Romans 14:10 (KJV Mod.). The real question before the church today is has God dealt with sin? The holiness movement apparently believes that God has not dealt with sin so they try to deal with the sin themselves. All I can say to this, is good luck, because you are under the law and as Paul said, *"Do you hear the law?"* Romans 4:21 (KJV Mod.).

Do you really understand what is required to be holy and fulfill the law? You must be like Christ. God will only accept perfection. It would be easier for us to jump across the Grand Canyon than to fill one iota of the law. And even if we did fulfill the law, it would not be acceptable to God, because we still have Adam's blood coursing through our veins. In other words, we are sinners in need of a Saviour.

It is not only the holiness that are in trouble. It's any religion that thinks they will be accepted by their good works or their own piety. These people are outside of Christ and even if they claim to be Christians, they are not. They are counterfeits. These are the ones that will say, *"Lord, Lord, have we not prophesied in your name? And in your name cast out devils and in your name done many wonderful works? And Jesus will say, "Depart from me, I never knew you."* Matthew 7:22-23 (KJV Mod.).

If you are one of these counterfeits, I would like to ask you now to repent of your religion. Give up your self-righteousness and cast yourself upon the mercy of God so that Christ can save you.

A rich young ruler came to Jesus. His question was, "What must I do to inherit eternal life?" Jesus pointed him to the law, because he knew that the rich man was self-righteous. Jesus said, "Do you know the commandments: do not commit adultery, do not steal, do not kill, do not lie, honor your father and mother?"

The rich young ruler said, "All these things I have kept from my youth up."

Guess what. The rich young ruler just broke the Fourth Commandment! He was too proud to admit that he was a sinner. Now, when Jesus heard these things, he said, "You lack one thing. Go sell all that you have and give it to the poor and you shall have treasure in heaven. Then come, follow me." And when he heard this, the rich man was very sorrowful, for he was very rich." (See Luke 18-18-22, KJV Mod.).

The ruler had failed again, because the law says, "Love your neighbor as yourself." Christ had tried to convince him again that he was a sinner, but to no avail. To begin with, the question is not what must we do to get eternal life. The question is: what has God done so that we might have eternal life? The rich and the proud always come to do and not to receive. For it is the gift of God that we need. We have nothing to offer.

Again, I would like to say, that to fulfill God's law, *'You must love God with all your heart, mind and strength.''* Deuteronomy 6: 4-6 (KJV Mod.) and *"love your neighbor as yourself."* Leviticus 19: 17-18 (KJV Mod.).

In the Old Testament, when an Israelite sinned, he had to bring a sheep or goat to the priest of the Tabernacle. It had to be a male animal, without a blemish, and the priest would kill the animal outside of the Tabernacle and then sprinkle the blood around the Tabernacle and on the altar where the animal would be dissected, washed and then burned. All of this points to Christ and his crucifixion. He was the Lamb of God for us. Scripture says *"The soul that sins must die."* Ezekiel 18:20 (KJV Mod.). This is the law. As the animals died in the place of the Israelite, so Christ takes our death for us in our name and on our behalf.

Some would have you believe that our sins were "imputed to Christ" and God punished Christ in our place. Not so. Christ never became sinful or a sinner. This is not correct doctrine. The crucifixion of Christ was a fulfillment of the law. A broken law requires payment or satisfaction.

Paul wrote, *"Christ has redeemed us from the curse of the law being made a curse for us, for it is written cursed is anyone that is hung on a tree."* Galatians 3:13 (KJV Mod.). Not only did Christ fulfill the law by his obedience, he also fulfilled the law for us by taking our curse.

It is as though the human race was sentenced to death because we had broken God's holy law. We are all guilty and the penalty is death. We are on death row, sentenced to die. This death is more than just physical death, it is eternal separation from God.

Jesus was the Lamb of God without spot or blemish. God accepts the righteous life and the death of Christ on our behalf and in our place. The law has been fulfilled and satisfied by Christ. This is how we are saved from the law. The resurrection is God's stamp of approval on the life and death of Christ on our behalf, for he truly did love us more than he loved himself.

Chapter 12
The Apostles' Doctrine and Hell

The Apostles believed in a real hell because Jesus taught it. It is also taught in the Old Testament. This is not a pleasant thing to teach; the thought of our unsaved loved ones going to a place of eternal punishment is something we would really not like to think about. I have probably struggled with this more than anyone. I most certainly don't like the idea of people going to hell regardless of what they believe, or don't believe. But I am not God, I don't make the rules. Nor am I able to comprehend just how holy God is.

I do know this: that Jesus came into the world to save sinners and he has accomplished all that is necessary for our salvation. His death on the cross should be a warning to all who reject him. This is very serious business. This was not a mere man hanging there on the cross, suffering there for us. No, this was God himself, manifested in the flesh. To turn your back on it, or to say you don't want it or need it makes me sure that there is a hell.

At one time, I thought God surely will not send anyone to hell for all eternity. Hell is probably a place where your soul is destroyed, that's it, you just kind of die. Unfortunately, I cannot find any scripture to verify this belief.

The Apostle Paul said next to nothing about hell. Of course, Paul's teaching was centered on grace, forgiveness and the Gospel. But even the teaching of the Gospel, there is a warning of eternal punishment. Even if you don't mention hell, there are words in the New Testament like: salvation, deliverance, redemption, grace, that tells us that there are words that are just the opposite of these words, even if they are not mentioned. It seems that everyone has the knowledge of hell. It seems to be one of the most widely used religious words in the English language. I'm constantly hearing people say, "To hell with this or that" or just simply, "Hell, no, or Hell, yes." I've never heard anyone say they wanted to go there. I know there are a lot of people that would like to send someone else there. I have had the invitation extended to me more than once! I simply declined.

In the book of Deuteronomy, the songs of Moses, there is an inkling that there may be various degrees of hell. Moses wrote *"For a fire is kindled in my anger and shall burn into the lowest hell."* Deuteronomy 32:22 (KJV Mod.).

Paul talks about his experiences of being caught up into the third heaven (II Corinthians 12:2). Perhaps there are various degrees of heaven and hell. There are several words for hell in the Old Testament. It is commonly called Shoal. Another word that Jesus used was Gehenna, which was a place outside of Jerusalem that was a dump where they burned refuse. The word Hades also means Hell.

Hell is always depicted as a place below, a place of torment and suffering. I quite frequently hear of near death experiences where people seem to rise outside of their bodies and go towards a light, which I assume, is heaven. But I've never heard of an experience where someone went to hell. Maybe there have been experiences like this, but they prefer not to talk about it.

The Bible depicts Hell as a place of fire and smoke. I don't think Hell was created for people. I think Hell was created for Satan and his angels, but through choice, people will go there also. I have heard some say that they would not be happy in heaven; that it's not a place that they would want to go to. They would like to believe that when you die, that's it. You just don't exist anymore. Sorry, but the Bible doesn't teach anything like that.

Paul wrote *"That we shall all stand before the judgment seat of Christ and every knee will bow and every tongue will confess to God so that every one of us should give account of himself to God."* Romans 14:10-12 (KJV Mod.).

The Lord will judge his own, not for sin, but for faithfulness to the Gospel. Those outside of Christ will be judged in their sins. A lot of unsaved people want to be cremated. Their thinking is that God will not be able to bring them back. I have bad news for them, if this is their plan. *"For in the twinkling of an eye, God will call you back and you shall stand before him in the Judgment."* 1st Corinthians 15: 52 (KJV Mod.). But for those that trust in Christ, there will be no judgment for sin.

In the teachings of Jesus, weeping and gnashing of teeth is mentioned seven times! Sometimes it is cast out where there shall be weeping and gnashing of teeth. Jesus told the parable about a king that made a marriage for his son and he sent his servants to call on them that were invited and they would not come. So he sent other servants to bid those that were invited. The king said everything is ready that I have prepared. Come to the marriage.' And those that were invited made light of it and killed his servants.

When the king heard this, he was angry and he sent his armies to kill those murderers and destroy their city. Then he said to the servants, go out and invite whoever will come to my son's marriage. The marriage was furnished with guests and when the king came to see the guest, the king noticed there was a man there without a wedding garment on and the king said, 'how did you get in without a wedding garment' and the man was speechless. Then the king said to his servants, 'bind him both hand and feet and cast him into outer darkness where there is weeping and gnashing of teeth. For many are called, but few are chosen.' (see Matthew 22:1-14).

The Gospel first went to the Jews, but they rejected Christ and the Gospel. When Paul took the Gospel to the Gentiles, he was actually taking the Gospel to the world. The man that came into the wedding without a wedding garment on is a counterfeit. The wedding garment represents the righteousness of Christ by which all who trust in him are covered.

The meaning of the parable is: don't show up in the judgment in your sins or you will be cast into outer darkness where there is weeping and gnashing of teeth. When we sin, we should think of it as a transgression or violation of God's holy law. This is what sin really is. A lot of people sin and think they have gotten away with it because they didn't get caught.

Jesus said, *"Beware of the sins of the Pharisee which is hypocrisy. For there is nothing covered that should not be revealed. Neither is anything hid that shall not be made known."* Luke 12:1-2 (KJV Mod.). The Pharisees did a lot of secret sinning. These were probably sins of the flesh like adultery or fornication. The Scribes and the Pharisees brought a woman to Jesus that had been caught committing adultery. They said to Jesus, "This woman should be stoned to death according to the law of Moses" hoping they would trap him. They said, "What do you say about this?"

Jesus stooped down in the midst of them and began to write something in the dirt. They again pressed him for an answer. Jesus said, "He that is without sin, let him cast the first stone." Then Jesus bent over again in the midst of them and began writing in the dirt again. One by one, beginning with the oldest, they quietly began to leave, until Jesus and the woman were standing alone.

What do you think Jesus was writing in the dirt? Could it have been the names of the women that the Pharisees had committed adultery and fornication with? Jesus said to the woman, "Where are your accusers? Has no man condemned you?"

She said, "No man, Lord."

Jesus said, "Neither do I condemn you. Go and sin no more." See John 8:3-11 (KJV Mod.).

Perhaps in the Judgment when those that are outside of Christ plead their innocence, there will be a huge movie screen that will show their sin for all to see. Like when Jesus wrote names in the dirt. *"All things are naked and open to the eyes of the Lord."* Hebrews 4:13 (KJV Mod.).

Secret sins? I don't think there is such a thing. If you are a Christian and there is secret sin in your life, it is best to confess it to the Lord. You will never be judged for it. It's just a good thing to get it out in the open with him. You don't have to confess it or make it known to anyone else, this is something between you and the Lord.

I don't believe in public confessions. I heard of a woman who during an emotional church service, stood up and confessed that she was having an adulterous affair with one of the deacons. This type of action serves no constructive purpose and can damage whole families. It is best to confess it to the Lord and repent from actions as this. Sin always has its consequences, which are much worse than the short-lived pleasure of the sin. We are all sinners. There are two kinds of sinners: saved sinners and lost sinners, or you might say, Christian sinners and religious sinners. We all fall

into one of these categories. One thing is certain, we have all trans-
gressed God's holy law. *"For by the law is a knowledge of sin."*
Romans 3:20 (KJV Mod.).

The question always comes up: "Can we be saved after death
or before the Judgment?" Catholics believe in a place called purgatory. This is a place that exists to purge those souls that are not
'pure enough' to go to heaven. In other words, they are almost
saved, but not quite. They must undergo the intense pain of long-
ing for God as punishment for their sins.

The purpose of purgatory is to make one pure and without sin
so they can go into the presence of the Holy God. There is nothing in the Bible about such a place. Not only that, it is contrary to
the Gospel and is Antichrist. As far as I am concerned, it is another one of those religious fairy tales that are so prevalent today.
have even heard of priests charging their parishioners thousands of
dollars to pray some loved one out of purgatory. They should be
arrested for extortion. But because it's a religious matter, they are
allowed to get away with it.

There is a parable about Lazarus and a rich man. Lazarus died
and went into Abraham's bosom, which is heaven. The rich man
died and went to hell. The rich man, being in hell, saw afar off that
Lazarus was in Abraham's bosom, and he cried out, "Father
Abraham, have mercy on me. Send Lazarus so he may dip the tip
of his finger in water and cool my tongue, for I am tormented in
this flame."

But Abraham said, "Remember in your life, you had all the
good things." In other words, you had no need of Christ or salvation. But Lazarus had trouble and discomfort, but now Lazarus is
comforted and you are in hell. Besides all this, there is a great gulf
between us so that you cannot come here and we cannot go there.
(See Luke 16:19-26 (KJV Mod.).

I know this is not pleasant to read this, but there is no second chance. You are either lost or you are saved. There is no in-between or purgatory. Jesus said, *"Enter in at the straight gate, for broad is the way that leads to destruction and many there be that go that way. Because straight is the gate and narrow is the way that leads to eternal life and few there be that find it."* Matthew 7:13-14 (KJV Mod.).

Religion is the broad way. It's the way that seems right to a man, but the end of his ways are death. (Proverbs 14:12 KJV Mod.). Jesus is the narrow way. It's the way that leads to eternal life, and few there be that find it.

The rich man said to father Abraham, "I have five brothers. Let me go tell them about this place of torment." Abraham said to him, "They have Moses and the Prophets. Let them hear them."

"No," said the rich man. "But if one came from the dead and went to them, they will repent."

Abraham said, "If they didn't listen to Moses and the Prophets, neither will they be persuaded though one has risen from the dead." (See Luke 16:28-31, KJV Mod.).

Sorry. No second chance. No purgatory. No warnings. Christ on the cross should be warning enough. And he arose from the dead. This should be convincing enough. No one knows what it is like to live without the spirit of God. God's spirit is in the world.

"By his spirit we live and have our being. Christ is the image of the invisible God. The first born of every creature. By him all things were created that are in heaven that are on earth visible and invisible whether they be thrones, dominions, principalities or powers. All things were created by him and for him and he is before all things and by him all things exist." Colossians 1:15-17 (KJV Mod.).

The Spirit of Christ will not be in Hell. There will be a total separation of Himself from those that are lost. No one can imagine what that is going to be like. In this life, the presence of the Lord is evident. Not only can we see it in nature or his creation, we can see it in people. The spirit of the Lord fills the earth. The unsaved benefit from his presence as well as the saved, but in Hell, there will be no spirit of Christ; no evidence of his presence.

The Scripture talks about darkness, being cast out into outer darkness. Quite frequently in the New Testament, Christ is represented as light. There will be no light in Hell; only darkness and separation. Perhaps this will make Hell what it is.

Chapter 13
The Apostles' Doctrine and Heaven

What is heaven? Heaven is a real place. It's a physical place. What kind of matter is heaven made of? We don't really know. However, there are some descriptions of the New Jerusalem in the Book of Revelations. The light of the New Jerusalem was like precious stones. A jasper stone, clear as crystal. The foundation of the New Jerusalem is made up of 12 layers, each layer being a precious stone. The gates of the City are pearls and the streets are made of pure gold (Revelation 21).

Jesus said that he saw Satan falling from heaven like lightening. See Luke 10:18 (KJV Mod.). The reason Satan was cast out of heaven was because he wanted to exalt himself above God. There was rebellion in heaven, so the Lord cast out Satan and his angels (see Isaiah 14: 12-14 (KJV Mod.). Satan's dwelling place is here on earth for now.

I would like to inform you that Satan is alive and well. If you don't think so, just listen to the evening news or pick up the local newspaper. We live in a fallen world that is controlled by the devil himself. (See Ephesians 6:12 (KJV Mod.). Our hope is to escape from this world and spend eternity in heaven with Christ.

I've given some serious thought about heaven. Does it exist now? Where is it? When Jesus was baptized, the Scripture says that *"The heavens were opened unto him and the Spirit of God descended and lit upon him like a dove."* Matthew 3:16 (KJV Mod.).

When Stephen was stoned, the Scripture says *"He looked up into heaven and saw Jesus standing at the right hand of God."* (See

Acts 7:56, (KJV Mod.). In the book of Acts, Peter went up on the rooftop to pray and *"He saw heaven open and a vessel descending on him like a great sheet held together at the four corners."* (See Acts 10:11 (KJV Mod.).

John wrote, *"I saw heaven opened and behold, there was a white horse, and he that sat upon it was called Faithful and True."* Revelation 19:11 (KJV Mod.). Paul on the road to Damascus said, *"Suddenly a light shone about him from heaven and Jesus spoke to him."* Acts 9:3-4 (KJV Mod.).

John said, *"A door was opened in heaven and a voice that spoke to him was like a trumpet talking to him."* Revelations 4:1 (KJV Mod.) Moses wrote, *"The Lord came down in a cloud and spoke to him."* Numbers 11:25 (KJV Mod.).

What am I getting at? I have a theory. It's only a theory; I can not prove it. But I believe that the whole earth is surrounded by heaven. The reason that we cannot see it, is because it's in a different dimension. Our eyes are made for this earth. We have earthly eyes and can only see earthly things. Jesus said to Nathaniel, *"You shall see the heavens open and the angels of the God ascending and descending upon the Son of Man."* John 1:51 (KJV Mod.).

Where is heaven? It's up there, but we can't see it. When we look up, all we see is clouds, stars or blue sky. But when Christ returns to this earth, he will come in the clouds and every eye will see him (Revelation 1:7 (KJV Mod.). *"For as the lightening come out of the east and shines into the west, so shall be the coming of Christ."* Matthew 24:27 (KJV Mod.). Then we will receive our heavenly eyes and we will be able to see all that Jesus has prepared for us.

Jesus said, *"You believe in God, believe also in me. In my Father house are many mansions. If it were not so, I would have told you so*

I go to prepare a place for you and I will come back again and receive you unto myself so that where I am, you may be there also." John 14:1-3 (KJV Mod.). This is our hope: to be with Christ in heaven.

Paul tells us about his experience about being caught up to the third heaven. He said he couldn't tell whether he was in the body or out of his body and he heard words that were unspeakable (2nd Corinthians 12:3-4). Perhaps what Paul was saying here was that there are not any words to describe what he had seen. Paul said, *"Eyes have not seen, nor ears heard, neither has it entered into the heart of man the things that God has prepared for him that love him."* 1st Corinthians 2:9 (KJV Mod.). I suppose that heaven is beyond our comprehension.

There are many references made about angels in both the Old Testament and New Testament. Angels appeared to Mary and Joseph, angels were present at the birth of Jesus. There were no angels present at his crucifixion, but there were many angels present at his resurrection.

Angels will be very active at the Second Coming of Christ and during the Tribulation period spoken of in the book of Revelation. One may ask, what are angels? They are heavenly beings that were created for God's pleasure. They apparently have a will of their own because there was rebellion in heaven and Satan, who must have been a prominent angel, was cast out with his followers.

We don't know much about angels but they are active in carrying out God's will. When we get to heaven we will have authority over them and judge them. (See 1st Corinthians 6:3 (KJV Mod.). Maybe this is what caused the rebellion in heaven. Satan didn't like the idea of God creating a race of humans that would have authority over him, so he rebelled. This is just another theory of mine.

When we are resurrected, we will receive our new bodies. That is, unless the Lord comes first before we die. The Apostles believed in the resurrection. Paul wrote, *"If there be no resurrection of the dead, then is Christ not risen? And if Christ is not risen then our preaching and your faith are in vain."* 1st Corinthians 15:13-14 (KJV Mod.).

I don't know about you, but I'm looking forward to receiving my new body. These bodies that we have now are subject to all kinds of diseases and problems. As a matter of fact, our bodies are made to die. As Paul said, *"In Adam, all die. But in Christ, shall all be made alive."* 1st Corinthians 15:22 (KJV Mod.).

"There are celestial bodies and terrestrial bodies, but the glory of the celestial is of one kind and the glory of the terrestrial one kind. It is one glory of the sun and another glory of the moon. There are different glories of the stars. So also is the resurrection of the dead. It is sown in corruption and it is raised in incorruption. It is sown in dishonor, and raised in glory. It is sown in weakness, it is raised in power. It is sown a natural body, it is raised a spiritual body. There is a natural body and there is a spiritual body. The first man, Adam, was made a living soul. The last Adam, Christ, was made a quickening spirit. First the natural, and then the spiritual. The first man was of the earth. The second man is the Lord from heaven.

As we have born the image of the earthly, so also shall we bear the image of the heavenly. Flesh and blood cannot inherit the kingdom of God. Neither does corruption inherit incorruption. We shall not all sleep, but we shall all be changed in a moment, in the twinkling of an eye at the last trump the trumpet will sound and the dead shall be raised incorruptible." 1st Corinthians 15:40-52 (KJV Mod.).

This life is the seed life. It is the life that goes into the ground. But the life that comes from the seed life is the abundant life. Jesus said, *"I have come that you might have life and you might have it more abundantly."* John 10:10 (KJV Mod.).

Some would have you believe that this is the abundant life here and now. It is abundant all right, abundantly sinful and full of trouble. Our new bodies will be heavenly bodies, they will never grow old, they will never get sick, they will never die. I'm not really sure what they'll be like, but I know that when Jesus came out of the tomb, Mary did not recognize him. She mistook him for the gardener. Later on, he apparently went right through the walls when he appeared to doubting Thomas and the other Apostles.

John wrote, *"Now we are the sons of God and it does not appear what we shall be like, but we know that when he appears, we shall be like him for we shall see him as he is."* 1st John 3-2 (KJV Mod.). Paul wrote, *"For if we have been planted together in the likeness of his death, we shall also be in the likeness of his resurrection."* Romans 5:5 (KJV Mod.).

The Bible doesn't say much about what life will be like in heaven. I think there is a reason for this. If we really knew what it was like, we wouldn't want to spend another day on this earth. Paul said, *"It is better for me to depart and be with Christ, but I know for your sake, it is better for you that I remain here with you."* Philippians 1:23-25 (KJV Mod.).

Those of us who are in Christ, should have no fear of death. Death is nothing more than a transition between one life and another. I doubt very much that we will remember our life here on this earth. If we do, it will probably be like a vague dream. No one remembers being in their mother's womb or their birth experience. I doubt very much if we will remember our death experience and our transition into eternal life.

John wrote, *"The Lord will wipe away the tears from our eyes and there will be no more death or sorrow nor crying, neither shall there be any pain. For the former things are passed away."* Revelation 21:4 (KJV Mod.).

The days that we spend on this earth are sinful and full of trouble. It seems that Christians have more problems and trouble in their lives than people who are not Christians. I've been perplexed about this, and have given it a great deal of thought. If we looked at the faithful in the Bible, even in the Old Testament, their lives are a mess. David was continually crying out to the Lord because of some mess he was in, either brought about by his own actions, or someone else's.

I have concluded that the Lord wants us to look forward to heaven. So how does he do that? What's the first thing you think about when your roof caves in or your dreams go up in smoke? If you are like me, and I think you are, we turn to the Lord and eternal life. So maybe it's supposed to be a little bumpy in this life. Maybe we are not to be too comfortable here. I have an ear tuned for the trumpet sound. As the song *The Solid Rock* says "When he shall come with trumpet sound, Oh may I then in him be found dressed in his righteousness alone, faultless to stand before the throne." (Edward Mote, c 1832 *The Solid Rock* Convention Press, Nashville, Tennessee).

Paul wrote, *"I reckon that the sufferings of this present life are not worthy to be compared to the glory that shall be revealed in us.* Romans 8:18 (KJV Mod.). Paul also said, *"Who shall separate us from the love of Christ? Shall tribulation or distress or persecution or famine or nakedness, or peril or sword? For your sake we are killed all day long. We are counted as sheep for the slaughter. In all things we are more than conquerors through him that loves us. For I am persuaded that neither death nor life nor angels nor principalities nor powers nor things to come nor height nor death nor any creature shall be able to separate us from the love of God which is in Christ Jesus our Lord."* Romans 8:35-39 (KJV Mod.).

Chapter 14
The Apostles' Doctrine and Religion

Religion is basically man's effort to become acceptable to God by what he has done or what he has become. It is man's effort to reach God, or man reaching out to God. In most of the religions of the world, men are building religious stairs that they hope will take them to God. These stairs are man made, man designed. You might say that they are "the way that seems right to a man." Religion is the natural way.

Religious people will say, "If I do this, or if I don't do that, I will be acceptable." Religion is always man-centered. All religions have their popes or their religion was founded by a man. In some religions, the founder claims that he had a "direct revelation from God," thus making him a spokesman for God.

It may be difficult to refute someone in this position. After all, he claims direct revelation from God. Are you going to argue with God? Religious people view God as holy and unyielding, making him like a taskmaster with his cracking whip ready to snap you on the back if you fail. There is little room for failure in religion. You must do what the Scripture says or you will be punished.

For years, I was told that if I didn't tithe, God would take it some other way. Yes, you must pay your dues or else. Obedience is mandatory in most religions. This is what makes religion what it is. Many religious people go to church so they can learn how to be more obedient. Some believe that the more obedient you are, the more blessings you will receive, or the more disobedient you are, the more curses you will receive. So you are always teetering back and forth between the blessings and the cursings. This is one horrible way to live, yet millions live this way. To be religious is to live under the law and the law says, 'do.'

I suppose that this is why religious people are so busy. Perhaps they are trying to please God with their busyness. Most churches have a full schedule of activities. You could probably spend most of the time down at the church if you wanted to. The priest and the pastors are busy, busy, busy, running to and fro doing what they think is the Lord's work.

I attended a wedding sometime ago. It was a Catholic wedding. At the reception, I approached the priest that had officiated at the wedding. I said to him, "Father, I have a question."

He said, "Yes, my son, what is it?"

I said, "How is it that the thief who died on the cross with Christ, being a sinner, and not having done any good works, went to paradise with Christ?"

He took two steps back from me and looked at me like I had just kicked him in his shins. I was also going to ask him about why the woman caught committing adultery was forgiven. When suddenly, he saw someone on the other side of the room that he had to talk to and left quickly, leaving me standing there with my questions unanswered.

I guess I have a reputation for antagonizing religious people. don't do it for the fun of it. I do it in hope that they will rethink their religious beliefs. Sometimes it's necessary to offend people in the hope that they will repent of their religion and come to Christ

Jesus called the Pharisees fools, blind guides, hypocrites, serpents, sons of hell, whitewashed tombs. The Pharisees were stunned by this. No man had ever talked this way to them! Most people in that day looked up to them and admired them. Jesus was trying to shock them into the reality that they were sinners.

If you don't know that you are sick, you can never go to the one that can heal you. As long as you think you are okay, you will never be saved. Jesus said he didn't come to call the righteous, but he came to call sinners (see Matthew 9:13, (KJV Mod.). Why not the righteous? Because they don't need him. Like the Pharisees, they didn't need him. But the prostitutes, tax collectors and other sinners welcomed Jesus and accepted him.

Religion can be a dangerous thing. Remember, it was the religious people that had Christ crucified. Religion is void of the spirit of Christ, therefore, it is capable of almost anything. Most of the problems in the world today are caused by religion. Religious people suffer from a severe case of mind-set. This is why they are so hard to reach with a liberating Gospel of Jesus Christ.

Can you imagine the Apostles trying to convince an old Pharisee that the religion that he had been doing for the last 40 years was wrong and that Jesus was his new Messiah and he was no longer under Moses' law? No wonder they wanted to kill them! Look at what happened to Stephen.

People hate change, especially when you have to change your mind about what you believe. Repentance doesn't necessarily mean turning from sin. Sometimes it means changing your mind about what you believe, like turning away from religion and turning to Christ and the Gospel. It is easier to reach someone with the Gospel who has never been religious than someone who has had a life of religion.

I was very religious before I knew the Gospel. It took years for me to accept all that Christ had done for me, but I kept searching, and little by little, bit by bit, the marvelous Gospel of Christ came through to me. A lot of the things that I thought were okay, I now question. The Gospel calls many religious practices into question simply because they are just that: religious practices.

When Christ died on the cross, the veil of the temple was torn from top to bottom. This veil separated the holy place from the Holy of Holies. This inner room in the Temple represented the very presence of God. When the high priest would go into the Holy of Holies and make an offering for the sins of the people, they would tie a rope around his ankles so that they could drag him out. Some of the priests apparently had unconfessed sin in their lives and when they would go into the Holy of Holies, they died.

When the veil was rent in two, it meant that we now have direct access to God in the person of Jesus Christ. This was the end of religion. No more priest to mediate between man and God. No more temples or sacrifices. No more laws or rituals. Christ is now our high priest who stands in the presence of God for us.

I know that a lot of Christians like to think that Jesus is all God but he is not. He is also human. He had to be human to save us. The point that I would like to make here is that our humanity is at the right hand of God. This is the essence of our salvation. Our salvation is sure because it is in heaven.

If you are religious, chances are your focus is Christ in your life or in your heart. Gospel believing Christians focus on Christ in heaven at the right hand of God. This is where our salvation is. Trying to figure out what Christ may be doing in your heart or your life can be a bit confusing. Because the old Adam is in there also. Once again, I must say, Christianity is an objective religion; we go outside of ourselves to another. The other being Jesus Christ, his life, his death and his resurrection. There is no strength in and of ourselves. Inward groveling or spiritual navel watching will only lead to a life of despair.

Again, I must say, religion is subjective; the Gospel is objective. Because religion is subjective, it is also subject to all sorts of problems; mainly that of false teachers who manipulate people through fear or emotion. Whereas the Gospel is a past, historical, one-time event.

A good example of religion and the Gospel is demonstrated when Cain and Abel brought their offerings to the Lord. We should keep in mind that offerings in the Old Testament pointed forward to when God would provide a Saviour. Christians now take the Sacraments, which points back to when God did provide a Saviour. We need to understand this to know why God was displeased with Cain's offering which was fruit and vegetables, and why the Lord was pleased with Abel's offering, which was a blood offering from one of the firstlings from his flock, which represented Christ's death on the cross. The fruits and vegetables represented religion, which came from Cain's work of tilling the ground and planting.

Another example is found in Leviticus 9: Moses called Aaron and his sons and the elders of Israel to prepare a burnt offering for the sins of the people. Now, the Lord appeared before Moses and the congregation and gave them explicit directions on how to prepare the burnt offerings and what should be done with the inward parts of the animal and the fat and the blood. This is very serious business, because it all pointed to Christ on the cross.

Aaron had two sons, Nadab and Abihu, and they were religious with ideas of their own on how this should be done. There are always some that would subvert the Gospel with their own ideas.

Scripture says that Nadab and Abihu took a pan and put fire in it and then they put incense into it and offered strange fire before the Lord. They had been commanded not to do this, but they did it anyway. Chapter 10:2 says that fire went out from the Lord and they both died before the Lord.

There are a lot of strange religions in the world today that have nothing or very little to do with Christ and his Gospel. To the Lord, this is like strange fire offered by Nadab and Abihu. It's not acceptable. Not then, not now. There is only one Gospel, there is only one way to believe. There is only one Christ. This is God's way, not man's way. Everything else is strange fire. Most of the religions in the world today are devised by man.

Thomas Jefferson said, "I don't find in orthodox Christianity one redeeming feature. The greatest enemies of Jesus are the doctrines and creeds of the church. It would be more pardonable to believe in no God at all than to blasphemy him with the atrocious writings of the theologians. John Calvin was a demon and a malignant spirit."

John Adams became so disenchanted with the religious baggage of Christianity that he wrote, "Nowhere in the Gospels do we find a precept for creeds, confessions, oaths, doctrines and a whole boat load of other foolish trumpery than we find Christianity encumbered with."

Abraham Lincoln said, "Christianity is not my religion. I can never give asset to the long, complicated statements of Christian dogma."

It is not God's will that there are so many denominations and different doctrines. Paul wrote to the Corinthians, "*I beseech you brethren that you all speak the same thing and that there be no*

divisions amongst you and that you be perfectly joined together in the
same mind and in the same judgments."   1st Corinthians 1:10
(KJV Mod.).

The reason Paul said this is because they wanted to start a new
denomination. Some wanted to split off and call their group the
First Church of Paul. Others wanted to call their church, The First
Church of Peter. (The Catholics finally succeeded in this). Others
said, "Wait, our church will be the first church of Apollos."
Another group said, "You are all wrong, our church will be the First
Church of Christ." (See 1st Corinthians 1:12, (KJV Mod.).

Which church would have been the right church? None of
them. Religion starts with organization. Then there has to be a
hierarchy, then a building. Paul rebuked them for wanting to do
this (verse 1-13). He said, "Was Christ divided? Was Paul crucified for you? Were you baptized in the name of Paul? Thank God,
I didn't baptize any of you!"

Again, I must say, religion causes division. The Gospel unites.
In the Gospel, we are all equal. In religion there is a struggle to be
better or greater. James and John came to Jesus with a request.
"Master." They said. "It is our request that when you come into
your glory, one of us should sit on your right hand and the other
on your left." (Mark 10:35-37). Verse 41 says that the other ten
disciples were displeased when they heard this. The account in
Matthew says that they were filled with indignation.

Jesus straightened them out by saying, "If you want to be the
greatest, you must be the servant of all." That was the end of their
attempt at religion. They wanted to set themselves above and apart
from the other disciples. Good try, but Christ wanted no part of it.
Neither should we have any part of someone who claims to be
greater or better. The spirit of Christ is the spirit of giving, not

receiving. Jesus said, "I didn't come to be ministered to, but to minister unto even to give his life as a ransom for many."

Jesus said to his disciples, take heed and beware of the leaven of the Pharisees. Leaven was an ingredient used in the baking of bread. He was not really talking about bread, Jesus was talking about the doctrine of the Pharisees. And what was the doctrine of the Pharisees? It was a religion of the book, or of the law. Religion thrives on laws and rules. Some of the largest cults are religions with very strict rules.

I remember when my mother was a member of the Pentecostal Church. It was considered a sin to drink a soft-drink out of a bottle, but it was okay to drink it out of a glass, but not out of a bottle. Remember, the Pharisees took the Ten Commandments and came up with over 630 rules to live by! Religious people love laws and rules. This is why they are religious.

Society needs laws and rules, because without them there would be chaos. We need to live in an orderly environment. But in our relationship with Christ, it's different. We obey him because we love him, not because we are commanded to. That would be religion. We love Christ because he first loved us in giving himself for us as our Saviour.

The Pharisees didn't really love the Lord. This is what made them hypocrites. I think they obeyed the laws and rules out of fear of going to hell. The Scripture says that "the soul that sins shall die" (meaning spiritual death.) They didn't believe that God would provide them with a Saviour. And if he did, they were going to be sure they didn't need him. Only sinners need a Saviour. The minute a person becomes religious, he becomes a hypocrite. The reason for this is no matter how holy we think we have become, we are still sinners.

Religion puts us at odds against God. Look at what the Pharisees did to the Son of God. The Gospel makes us friends with God. Religion is Antichrist. The Gospel is peace and grace. Religion says 'do.' The Gospel says, 'done."

No one likes to be told what to do. We are all rebellious. That's why the Lord came to do something for us, not to give us laws and rules, but to take away the laws and rules. Now we can be friends with God. Have you ever noticed a good friend doesn't boss you around? If you want to make enemies, just start bossing them around. Soon they will hate you with a passion. This is what was wrong with the Pharisees; God was the boss, you better do the rules, or else, they thought. It was blessing if you were obedient and cursing if you were not.

Children obey parents much better if they truly feel they are loved. We are no different. We feel we want to be obedient to Christ because we know that he loves us. There was no grace in the doctrine of the Pharisees. The law said, 'do.' The only grace the Jews can come up with is the Passover that took place in Egypt. And even this points to the saving work of Christ. Obedience follows love. They are like companions. Take away the love and you have pure rebellion.

I think this is what happens to teenage children. They reach a stage when they are no longer dependent upon their parents for love and caring, and in the process of becoming independent adults, they want fewer rules and more freedom. Instead, they get just the opposite. What's the solution? I don't know. Every case is different. All I can say is you should make a tremendous effort to love them and show some grace and forgiveness. Grace and forgiveness go a long ways.

Paul wrote, *"Because the law brings wrath for where there is no law, there is no transgression. Therefore, it is of faith that it might be by grace."* Romans 4:15-16 (KJV Mod.). *"To be under the law, or to be religious is to be under the wrath of God. Being justified by his blood, we should be saved from wrath through him."* Romans 5:9 (KJV Mod.).

I strive not to be religious. I don't do the Sacraments, even though I have the freedom to do them. I do not observe any religious holidays. Sunday is just another day. I do not attend any church nor do I belong to any denomination or special group. I guess if someone was to observe me, they would probably think I'm an atheist. Of course, that is not true. I just do not practice religion. I see no need to do these things. All that matters to me is that God has accepted Jesus Christ on my behalf and now I have entered into his rest. As the Scripture says, *"He that has entered into his rest has also ceased from his own works."* Hebrews 4:10 (KJV Mod.).

I am not writing this book to please God. I am writing this book so that others may enter into his rest also. Religion is an enemy of the Gospel and it is Antichrist. I enjoy taking a shot at it every time I get a chance, in the hope that someone may see the error of their way and turn to Christ and his Gospel.

God's Word is the final authority. It's the Word that he gave to Adam; the directions for building the ark that he gave to Noah, the Word he gave to Abraham, the Word that he gave to Moses in the building of the Tabernacle. Jesus Christ is the Word of God Incarnate. Everything is done and completed by the Word of God.

Jesus Christ is all that God willed him to be. You might say that Christ is the very mind of God. The voice from heaven said, *"This is my son in whom I am well pleased."* The church is not the authority. Christ did not legislate authority to the Apostles. The Apostles were to be ambassadors for Christ. Christ said, *"Go and teach all nations, baptizing them in the name of the Father, and of the Son, and the Holy Spirit, and teach them to observe all the things that I have commanded you."* Matthew 28:19-20 (KJV. Mod.).

The Apostles were to teach what they had learned from Christ and the Prophets. Religion takes the things of God and molds it to fit its own image of God, which it has set in it's own mind. In other words, religion tries to make God into it's own image, which is nothing more than an extension of itself. An ambassador represents the government that sent him. The ambassador does not impose his own laws or project his own ideas. He represents only the will of his government that sent him. Religion is basically man's idea of what God should be.

Martin Luther said, "I want the pure, unadulterated Scriptures in all their glory, undefiled by the comments of any man, even the saints, and not hashed up with any earthly seasonings, but you 'the school men' are the very people who have not avoided profane and vain babblings (to use Paul's words, 1st Timothy 6:20) and have wanted to cover these holy and divine delicacies with human glosses and pep them up with earthly spices and like Ezekiel (Ezekiel :12) my soul is nauseated in having to eat bread baked with human dung. Do you know what this means? The Word of God, when added to the word of man, serves as a veil to the pure truth. Nay, worse as I have said, it is the human dung with which the bread is baked. As the Lord figuratively expresses it in Ezekiel." This was Martin Luther's answer to Latomus. *Library of Christian Classics,* Philadelphia Westminster Press, Volume 16, p. 344-345.

Religion is Antichrist. It's purpose is to confuse the Word of God by adding the word of man and mixing it together so it is like the bread baked with human dung. There is only one Christ, there is only one Gospel. Antichrist will do what it can to keep you from knowing the truth about Christ and the Gospel. Since Christ is the final and complete Word of God to the human race, it is the work of Antichrist to degrade and dethrone Christ and make the Word of God of no effect. It does this by placing other things in front of or ahead of Christ and the Gospel.

Why are there so many different denominations? Are they divided over what the Gospel is? No. They are divided over religious practices. I have been to churches where Christ was seldom preached because the pastor spent most of his time preaching or defending the religious practices of the church. Or, he was preaching about the Christian life and how to live the victorious Christian life, which is not really very victorious at all. This is how Antichrist works. It is very subtle, and deceiving. It is the responsibility of the Christian to detect the spirit of Antichrist and he does this by testing the spirit in the light of the Gospel.

Chapter 15
The Gospel and Pentecostalism

Since this is a worldwide phenomenon, I thought it might be good to examine this as a separate issue of religion. Pentecostals can be found in almost any denomination. But it is most prevalent in the Roman Catholic Church.

The Pentecostal movement started in the early 1900's. Charles Parham joined with forty other persons in Kansas to seek the Pentecostal baptism of the Spirit. After several days of persistence, one by one, claimed that they had received the Baptism of the Spirit. Speaking in tongues was a guarantee that this experience was valid. W.J. Seymour led this experience in California. Other Pentecostal meetings were breaking out throughout the country.

In the years that followed, Pentecostals were not accepted into mainline denominations. In spite of the opposition, Pentecostalism grew to about eight million by 1960. Since then, it has infiltrated all denominational barriers. The main focus of this movement is the baptism of the Holy Spirit, with the evidence of speaking in tongues. There are many problems with this religion.

John wrote, *"When he, the Spirit of Truth has come, he will guide you into all truth, for he shall not speak of himself. But whatever he hears, that shall he speak. He will show you things to come. He shall glorify me (meaning Christ) for he shall receive of me and reveal it to you."* John 16:13-14 (KJV Mod.). The Scripture says that the Holy Spirit does not speak of himself. In other words, it does not draw attention to itself, nor will it draw attention to the one who possesses the Spirit.

Speaking in tongues is a showy thing. Even some of the cults claim that they speak in tongues.   Mormons and Jehovah Witnesses claim that some of them speak in tongues. The tongues that were spoken on the day of Pentecost were languages. They were either Greek or Aramaic. The purpose of this was so that every man could hear about the wonderful works of God, which was the Gospel.

The purpose of the Holy Spirit is to glorify Jesus Christ. Pentecostals have turned it around so that it glorifies them. Do they talk about Christ when they speak in tongues? Do they talk about the Gospel? No, they do it to be seen of men. Is there some new revelation from God outside of the Bible that they can reveal to us? Of course not. Then why do they do this?

One of the worst religious sins is pride and arrogance. Pride and arrogance are at their peek when someone claims that they have a gift that no one else has. Or that they have a special revelation from God that no one else has. Towards the end of the 19th century, many people within the holiness movement began to seek the baptism of fire. This was apparently taken from Acts 2 where it said that cloven tongues of fire sat over the Apostles.

One branch of this holiness movement was called the Fire Baptized Holiness Church. Those receiving the baptism of fire would fall down, scream, shout or go into a trance. The baptism of fire was regarded as the ultimate experience. After receiving the baptism of fire, you were then completely sanctified and ready for heaven. If this is the way it is, then Christ lived and died in vain.

To say that Pentecostalism is a subjective religion, may be an understatement. The problem is that the Apostles' religion was objective. They preached Jesus Christ crucified, risen and ascended to the right hand of God. They did not say anything about being baptized by the Holy Spirit after the day of Pentecost. No, their focus was on what Christ had accomplished on behalf of sinners.

Where do the Pentecostals get this theology of the spirits manifestation of tongues, fire, revelations, miracles, and so on? They didn't get it out of the Bible, because there is nothing in the Bible to validate this. This is Satan's plan to divert one's attention away from the Gospel and to themselves. This is a very clever plan. And it's working. People are more preoccupied by their own spirituality than they are with Christ and his Gospel.

There is no strength in a subjective religion. The more you look unto yourself for some manifestation of the spirit, the more discouraged you will become. Christianity is an objective religion. We go outside of ourselves to Christ and his Gospel. This is what the Apostles taught and this is what we should believe. Inward groveling and spiritual navel watching will produce very weak Christians.

Look at the history of the Pentecostal preachers. They have no strength in their lives because of their introverted religion. Strength comes from knowing that God has dealt with our sins in the person of Jesus Christ.

Pentecostalism is closer to eastern religion than it is to the Protestant religion. Most of the eastern religions are very subjective. That is, you go into yourself to find God. The deeper you go, the more real God becomes. This is a form of mysticism. Some followers of eastern religion actually go into a trance and they experience all kinds of inward sensations. Pentecostalism basically does the same thing.

How many times have you seen a group of Pentecostals with their hands held high and eyes closed thinking that they are feeling the Holy Spirit? When in reality, they are only feeling their own emotions. Again, I must say, that the Holy Spirit was given to bring honor and glory to Jesus Christ, not to give us some kind of tingling feeling right down to the balls of our feet. It is a grave error to confuse the Holy Spirit with human emotion.

Pentecostalism is a very emotional religion. You can even call it the religion of emotion. Without a highly charged emotional meeting, they will attest to you that the Holy Spirit was absent. The more frenzied the meeting, the more commotion, the more the Spirit was there. This is where they first got the name, "Holy Rollers." Because people would get so charged up they would fall down and start rolling around on the floor. Thus the name, "Holy Rollers."

Pentecostalism is a religion of the flesh. Paul wrote, *"For they that are after the flesh do mind the things of the flesh. But they that are after the Spirit, the things of the Spirit."* Romans 8:5 (KJV Mod.) The things that are after the Spirit, are the things about Christ. We no longer need tongues, miracles or revelations. We now have the complete revelation of Christ in the Bible. There is no need for manifestations of the Spirit to confirm that Jesus is the Christ.

When Paul wrote what he wrote in 1st Corinthians about the various manifestations of the Spirit, we should keep in mind, that they did not have a New Testament Bible then like we have now. Not only that, but Paul tried to play down speaking in tongues. He even said that tongues would cease (see 1st Corinthians 13:8) Paul said, *"What if you all come together in one place and you all start speaking in tongues. And what if there are unbelievers there or unlearned? Will they not think you are all nuts?"* 1st Corinthians 14:23 (KJV Mod.).

God is not speaking to us today in tongues or revelations

Nothing is being added to the Bible. There is no further word from heaven. All that we will ever need to know has been revealed to us in Christ. He is the Word of God. It's the Spirit's work now to show us all that he has accomplished on our behalf. Tongues and revelations are a thing of the past. They only distract from this marvelous work that Christ has done for us.

The Corinthian church was a troubled church. In First Corinthians, Paul is continually correcting them. The church is full of division and controversy. In one instance, it got so bad that Paul spoke out and said, *"I determine to know nothing among you, save Jesus Christ and him crucified."* 1st Corinthians 2:2 (KJV Mod.).

Apparently the Corinthian church was going in so many directions that Paul was completely frustrated. He even thought about beating them with a rod when he said, *"Shall I come to you with a rod or shall I come to you in love and in the spirit of meekness."* He simply didn't know how to approach them. (See 1st Corinthians 4:21, KJV Mod.).

1st Corinthians, Chapter Five tells about a man that has had sex with his father's wife, which would have been his stepmother. Paul said, "You are puffed up about this. No one is sorry about it. Why didn't you put this fellow out of the church?" Verse six indicates that they were glorying about this matter.

Of all of the churches that Paul wrote to, the Corinthian church was the most troubled. Why was this so? Because they had an internalized religion. They were more interested in speaking in tongues than they were in Christ and his Gospel. The same thing is true today. People are more interested in their own spirituality than they are in Christ and the Gospel.

There are many television evangelists today that will tell you that if you believe you can have a miracle in your life. These same evangelists will also tell you that if you send them money, it will be like planting a seed and from this seed a blessing or miracle will come from it. They usually display a stack of testimonial letters to verify that this is indeed really happening. They should be arrested for extortion. There is nothing in the Bible that condones this practice. They are simply taking advantage of the poor and the ignorant. Not only is this not scriptural, it is criminal. Why the Federal Communication Commission doesn't do something about it is a mystery to me.

Why did Jesus perform miracles? The miracles that Jesus did were to confirm that he was who he claimed to be. Nicodemus understood this when he said that no man can do these miracles that you do unless God is with him (see John 3:2).

Jesus did miraculous works, not to glorify himself as a great healer, but to confirm that he was indeed the Christ, the Saviour of the world. Not only did he confirm that he was the Christ, but he showed great love and compassion to the people that he healed. Performing of miracles was a sign to the Jews that this was the Messiah.

Some Jews came to Jesus to trap him and said to him, "How long will you make us doubt if you are the Christ, tell us plainly." Jesus answered them, *"I told you, and you don't believe me. The works that I do in my Father's name, they bear witness to me."* John 10:24-25 (KJV Mod.).

What about the miracles that were performed by the Apostles? One of the first miracles was performed by Peter and John at the Temple. There was a man there who had been crippled all of his life. Peter looked upon him and said, "In the Name of Jesus Christ get up and walk." Peter took him by his right hand and lifted him up. The man stood and went leaping and jumping and praising God. They entered into the Temple and all the people saw him and knew that he had been crippled all of his life.

At the right time, when a great crowd had gathered, Peter said, "Why are you looking at us like we performed this miracle by our own power or holiness?" And what did Peter do then? He directed them to Jesus Christ and what he had done for them. Peter lifted up Christ. This miracle confirmed that what the Apostles said was from God, and was true. Every time the Apostles performed a miracle, the same thing took place. They lifted up Christ and preached the Gospel.

Do Pentecostals do this when they claim they have performed a miracle? The answer is no. The question is, is God performing miracles today? If he is, I haven't seen one. Why are all the miracles the Pentecostals claim are happening are somewhere else; like out of sight? Why is it that they are not down at the hospitals healing people and emptying hospital beds?

When the Apostles did a miracle, there was no question about it. It was an authentic miracle. There was no partial healing or patch-up healing. Everyone wants to see a sign or a miracle today. Jesus said, *"A wicked and adulterous generation seeks after a sign, but no sign shall be given except the sign of Jonah."* Matthew 16:4 (KJV Mod.).

The sign of Jonah pointed to Christ's death and resurrection. The greatest miracle has already taken place. When God gave us Christ, it was the miracle of all miracles. Nothing compares to it. The world was turned upside down by the Christ event. Millions have been changed because of Jesus Christ. In all the history of the world, nothing compares to the Christ event. Even if you are not a believer, you would have to admit that Jesus Christ has had more of an impact on the world than any other person.

The reason there are not any miracles today is because we now have a complete revelation of him in the Bible. God doesn't want to take away from this awesome event that took place more than 2,000 years ago. The Scripture says *"In these last days, God has spoken to us by his Son."* Hebrews 1:2 (KJV Mod.).

All that we need to know has been revealed in Jesus. He is God's final message to the world. No more signs. No more revelations or miracles. If you want a sign or miracle, you will have to wait for the Antichrist to appear. The Antichrist will do some great miracles, even causing fire to come down from the sky upon the earth. I'm not going to be here to see it, but the Scripture said that many will be deceived because of it. (See Revelation 13:13-14) Their end is the lake of burning fire. (See Revelation 19:20).

In the light of all of this, we can only conclude that Pentecostalism is not according to the Gospel of Christ, but is Antichrist because they place a greater emphasis on their experience over and above the experience of Christ and his Gospel. The Gospel of Christ is objective for it points the sinner to something which is completely outside of his own experience.

Chapter 16
Christ and
The Old Testament

Right after Adam and Eve sinned, God promised them a Saviour. We don't really know if they believed that God would provide a Saviour, nor do we know if they would accept a Saviour. The Bible doesn't say. Even though God promised them a Saviour, the curse was not taken away and still remains today. We live in a fallen world and we are all members of a fallen race.

The fall of Adam was much worse than what we realize. Because of the fall, the whole human race is infected with sin. Everyone born after Adam is a sinner. No one likes this idea of being a sinner, but there is nothing we can do about it. It is best to accept it and try not to act out the sinful desires.

Early civilization became so corrupted that God said that he was sorry that he had ever created man. So God decided to destroy his creation and start over again. (Genesis 6:5-7). But there was one man that found favor with God. His name was Noah. The Scripture says that Noah was a just man that walked with God.

God instructed Noah in the building of the Ark. When the Ark was finished, Noah and his family and two of every kind or animals entered into the Ark and God sealed the door. The Ark was a picture of Christ. All who are in Christ are saved. The Holy Spirit is the seal. We are sealed by his Spirit. This is our sanctification.

Next is Abraham. Abraham always did what God told him to do, no matter what it was. He obeyed God without question.

Abraham had perfect faith and trust in the Lord. Abraham was the father of the Jewish nation and the Arab nation.

Another picture of Christ was found in the almost sacrifice of Isaac on Mt. Moriah. Abraham was the beginning of the Jewish nation. God would bring forth a people and a nation and from this people and nation, there would be the Saviour of the world. This was God's plan. It did not just happen. The Old Testament is about the people who played a part in this plan of redemption.

There is a genetic line in the Old Testament that leads to Christ. This can be found in the first Chapter of Matthew. This genetic line along with all the prophecies about Christ ties the Old Testament and the New Testament together. They both complement each other. They both tell us about Christ. The Old Testament is not a book for the Jewish religion, it is a book for the Christian religion. Christ is everywhere in the Old Testament, but we must seek it out and look for it. In the Old Testament, they looked forward to the Saviour. We look back. We are all saved by faith.

Moses was most certainly a picture of the Saviour in that he was instrumental in leading the Jews out of bondage and into freedom. The Passover also speaks of Christ; the blood of the Lamb over the doorway of the Hebrew houses speaks of Christ and his atonement on the cross.

The Tabernacle worship was established by Moses according to the instructions given by God. Almost everything about this Tabernacle pointed to Christ, even the priests that officiated in the Tabernacle are types of Christ (see Hebrews Chapter 5).

Just because the Jews are blind to this, doesn't mean that we should be blind to it. All of the offerings that took place at the

Tabernacle pointed to the Saviour. Even the giving of the law is about Christ, because Christ was the embodiment of the law. The fiery serpent (that Moses placed on a pole so that everyone that looked upon it was healed from their snake bites) speaks of Christ's redemptive work on the cross.

King David was very Saviour conscious. The Psalms are full of words like salvation, redeemer. Again, we must read the Old Testament with Christ in mind. One of the most graphic pictures of Christ is found in the 53rd Chapter of Isaiah. There are also many other Scriptures in this book that speak of Christ. Jonah's experience with the whale is a description of the death and resurrection of Christ. The word salvation is used over one hundred times in the Old Testament. Salvation means to be saved from something; usually from the consequences of sin.

One thing we should keep in mind when reading the Old Testament as well as the New Testament is that it was written under the law. Remember the law says, 'do' and the Gospel says 'done.' Christ is the fulfillment of the Old Testament and the conclusion of the New Testament. The Old Testament points to Christ. Unfortunately, the Jews missed this. Instead they got hung up on the law and religion.

Both the Old and New Testament portray God as the judge. It is the work of the judge to make judgments. God is the just judge or the righteous judge. Righteousness and judgment are the habitation of his throne (see Psalm 97:2 (KJV Mod.). When God makes a judgment, he makes it by his word. Paul wrote, *"For the word of God is quick and powerful and sharper than any two edged sword, piercing, even to the diving asunder of this soul and spirit and of the joints and marrow and is the discerner of the thoughts and intents of the heart."* Hebrews 4:12 (KJV Mod.).

When Adam and Eve sinned, God found them guilty and pronounced the judgment for violating his holy law. Not only is he the just judge, he is the merciful judge in that he promised them a Saviour. When God makes a covenant or a promise as a result of his judgment, he does it in righteousness.

David wrote, *"I will praise you O Lord, you have sat on the throne judging righteously. You have rebuked the nations and destroyed the wicked. You have blotted out their name forever. The Lord reins forever. He has established his throne for judgment. He will judge the world in righteousness. He will govern the peoples with justice."* Psalm 9:1,4,5,7,8 (KJV Mod.).

When God promised Adam and Eve a Saviour, it was a donedeal. It was not a question of whether or not it would happen. It was simply a matter of when. God is just and he is merciful. Love and mercy are related words in the Bible, because he loves us, he is merciful. Otherwise, we would not have a Saviour. We are blessed because our God is truthful and keeps his promises and is just and merciful in his judgments. Because of this, we can trust in him and in his word.

The patriarchs believed in the righteous judgments of God. They believed that all that God said was right and true. They believed God. They were saved by believing God. We are saved the same way, by faith in God's word and in God's promises. God says that Jesus is the Saviour. If we don't believe that, we cannot be saved, because we cannot believe God.

God is a God of judgment. All of his ways are judgment. (See Deuteronomy 32: 4, KJV Mod.). All of the great acts of God in the Old Testament, the flood, the Exodus, were all acts of God's judgment. They pointed forward to the future when God would judge the whole world in the death and resurrection of Christ. Jesus said, *"For judgment I have come into this world that they that see will see and those that don't see will be made blind."* John 9:39 (KJV Mod.).

The death of Christ was God's judgment for sin and a broken law. The terms of the covenant must be executed. Christ bore our curse (see Galatians 3:11-13, KJV Mod.).

There is no greater work in the history of humanity than the work of Christ. Because of this great redemptive work that Christ has done, God has exalted him and has given him a name above every name (see Philippians 2:10, KJV Mod.).

All authority and all power have been given unto him. Jesus is now Lord.

About the Author

Robert Pate is a bold witness for Jesus Christ. At one time he was affiliated with Christians in Action which is a small group of Christians that did street witnessing for Jesus Christ. Armed with a bible and a Christian tract, he would confront people on the streets of Los Angeles with the message of Jesus Christ.

He has previously been active in the organized church. His ministries included adult Sunday School teacher, Children's Church leader, Sunday School teacher for junior boys, bus captain, and visitation and teaching in rest homes and hospitals. He was also very active in the outreach and visitation ministry of his church.

Robert's interest in early Christian history led him to the discovery of the Apostles' Doctrine. Studying with Christian scholars for over 30 years has grounded him in the historical Gospel of Jesus Christ and all that this Gospel calls into question. Because of what he has learned, he is no longer welcome to teach in the organized church.

Robert is now retired and continues to study the historical Gospel of Jesus Christ. He lives in Eau Claire, Wisconsin with his wife of 35 years.

For additional copies of this book, write:
Robert E. Pate Publishing Co.
PO Box 62
Eau Claire, WI 54702
Fax 715-830-0453

Add $2.00 to the price of the book
for shipping and handling.
Cheque or Money Order only.